WHALEBACK SHIPS

AND THE

AMERICAN STEEL

BARGE COMPANY

WHALEBACK SHIPS

AND THE

AMERICAN STEEL

BARGE COMPANY

C. Roger Pellett

Wayne State University Press
Detroit

ISBN 978-0-8143-4476-7 (hardcover)
ISBN 978-0-8143-4477-4 (ebook)

Library of Congress Control Number: 2018930304

Wayne State University Press
Leonard N. Simons Building
4809 Woodward Avenue
Detroit, Michigan 48201-1309

Visit us online at wsupress.wayne.edu

Frontspiece: Whaleback steamship SS *Meteor* arriving in the Twin Ports of Duluth, Minnesota, and Superior, Wisconsin, late in her active career, c. 1969. Source: Superior Public Museums

CONTENTS

Plates follow page 82

LIST OF TABLES

Preface

Many people who live near the Great Lakes have heard of the whalebacks, those unusual ships invented by Duluth entrepreneur Alexander McDougall. Fewer people realize that one of these remarkable vessels still exists 120 years after her launch. She is the SS *Meteor*, launched in 1896 as the *Frank Rockefeller*. She hauled a variety of cargos around the lakes for over seventy years until she returned to Superior to become a museum ship. She is now berthed less than a mile from where she was built and is open to visitors each summer.

My involvement with the *Meteor* began in 2005 when I volunteered to join a small group of interested people to discuss plans for future preservation efforts. This soon developed into a project to document the *Meteor*'s remarkably intact triple expansion steam propulsion plant. Typical of the machinery that once powered shipping on the lakes, the *Meteor*'s propulsion plant is one of the very few still accessible to visitors.

My next project was to document the history of the ship herself and to identify the many changes made over the years to keep her competitive in the many trades in which she operated. Both my *Machinery Report* and *Meteor* history were donated to Superior Public Museums, the manager of the *Meteor* Whaleback Museum.

As I dug deeper into *Meteor*'s history, I began to realize that the events surrounding the building of the whaleback ships and the formation and demise of the company that built them made a remarkable story. This book is the result of my research; it focuses on the congruence of engineering and business and how the two interact to influence the success or failure of an enterprise.

When I began my engineering career many years ago, this concept would have been obvious to most readers. Engineers played a key role in mobilizing American business to defeat the Axis Powers in World War II, and twenty years later engineers were making it possible for America to win the space race with the Russians. With the decline of traditional manufacturing, however, that connection between engineers and business seems more tenuous with each passing year.

Unless built for military or recreational use, ships are economic entities, engineered to haul cargos profitably or to otherwise serve the owner's needs at the lowest possible cost. The whaleback barges and steamships built by the American Steel Barge Company worked in both of these roles: first as units of an independent steamship company, attempting to haul bulk cargos consigned by various owners at a profit, and second as part of the dedicated transportation system of a major iron ore producer.

The company attempted to diversify by building vessels for saltwater commerce, by building a passenger vessel, and by building whaleback steamships for the Great Lakes package trade, but these efforts either produced unsuccessful results or did not lead to hoped-for future business. These attempts at diversification were aspects of its business strategy, taken to achieve its overall goals as a "construction and transportation company." In the end, though, diversification was a distraction from the company's core business of delivering bulk cargos of ore, coal, and grain to customers around the Great Lakes. While accounts by many historians chronicle the supposed success of the *C. W. Wetmore*'s saltwater voyage or the opulence of the whaleback passenger steamer *Christopher Columbus*, this book instead discusses the role that they played in the company's success or failure.

Many aspects of ship design involve features that affect a ship's building or operating costs, and here engineering and business converge. The amount of cargo carried within a hull of given dimensions, the ease at which cargo can be loaded or unloaded, the cost to improve accessibility to the cargo hold, and the efficiency of the vessel's machinery plant are all examples of where the ship's designer is required to be both engineer and financial analyst.

Naval architects are responsible for producing ships that will be safe when subjected to the hazards of wind and water, and the designers of the whalebacks produced vessels that were seaworthy for the Great Lakes conditions that were familiar to them. Although several whaleback ships were lost to navigational hazards, no whaleback barge or steamship while operated by the American Steel Barge Company was sunk by weather conditions, therefore, shipwrecks are not a theme of this book. Later owners lost many whalebacks in trades that they were not designed for, or because of ill-advised modifications. These accidents, many tragic, are covered briefly in the epilogue, but they are largely beyond the scope of this book.

Ships are the largest moving objects built by man, and in the 1890s they were the most complex. For hundreds of years, ships of surprising size were built by artisans using only their "eye" and a rule of thumb. This was possible when these vessels were built from wood and propelled by oar or sail. The whalebacks and other first-class barges and steamships built on the Great Lakes during the 1890s were built from steel and propelled by steam. Steel plate and structural materials had to be fabricated in a workshop before final assembly on the launchways, and steam power plants required careful design. This required hundreds of drawings prepared by skilled marine drafts-men working under the direction of trained (and increasingly university-educated) naval architects and marine engineers.

In his autobiography Alexander McDougall, the whaleback ship's inventor, mentions only three types of individuals: his personal friends, the Eastern capitalists who financed the company, and those he believed had caused him to lose his investment. The talented men who ran the company for him are not mentioned. Furthermore, his claim that the first whaleback barge was built by unskilled stevedores and lumberjacks leaves us to assume that subsequent whaleback ships were built in the same manner. One recently published account even portrays McDougall at his drawing board, holding a T-square, wearing a green eyeshade, and personally designing ships. The author of this book has obviously never been trained in the art and skill necessary to produce accurate ship drawings, and neither was Alexander McDougall!

The only historian to identify any of the American Steel Barge Company's middle managers was historian Richard Wright in his book *Freshwater Whales*. I have tried to complete the picture by introducing readers to the talented, well-trained, and, in some cases, university-educated team of naval architects, marine engineers, and ship draftsmen—the men who were somehow convinced to venture to the Twin Ports of Duluth, Minnesota, and Superior, Wisconsin, at the edge of the great north woods, to make Alexander McDougall's dream of building whaleback ships a reality.

Unlike warships, successful merchant ships are usually not involved in dramatic events. Most go about their lives without drama, hauling the cargos that feed the economy. The statistics that measure this activity are a part of their story. Readers unfamiliar with the metrics of the shipping business may wish to read appendices A and B.

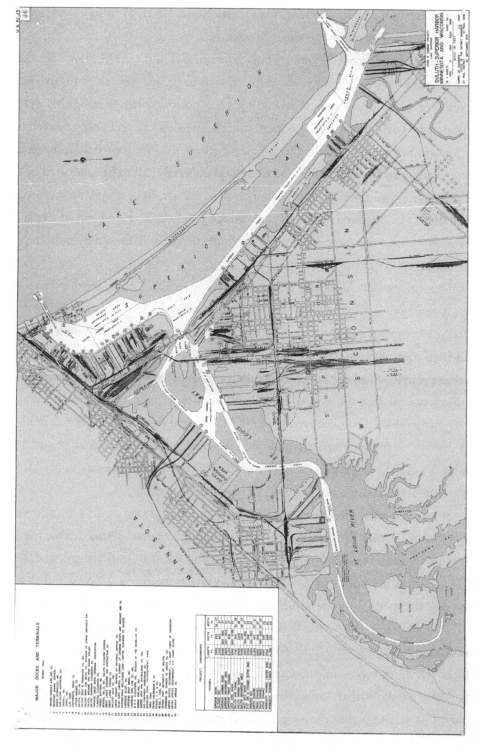

Map of Duluth–Superior Harbor. Source: U.S. Army Corps of Engineers.

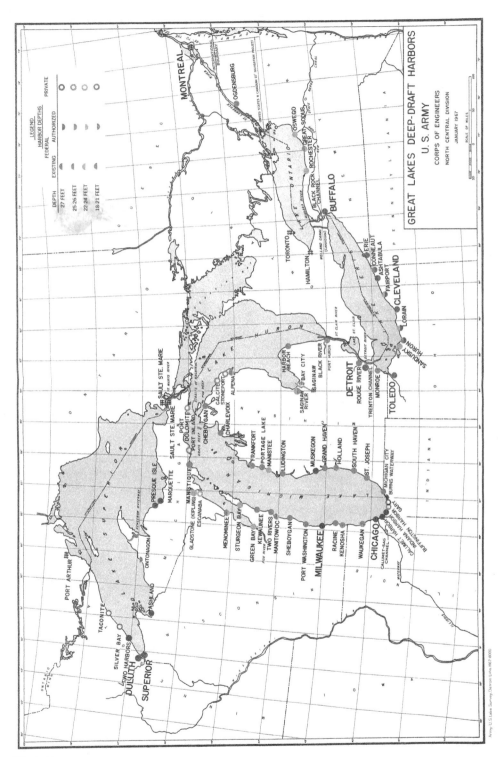

Map of the Great Lakes. Source: U.S. Army Corps of Engineers.

ACKNOWLEDGMENTS

This book was a team effort, and I would like to thank those who helped me make its publication possible.

First and foremost, I would like to thank Sara Blanck, Executive Director of Superior Public Museums, and Margaret (Maggie) Scheibe of the Superior Public Museums staff. Sara encouraged me to turn my whaleback ship research into a finished book manuscript and generously made the resources available to help me do so. Maggie served as editor-in-chief, organizing my manuscript, assembling the data necessary for submittal to prospective publishers, and reorganizing notes, text, and bibliography into the required format and required literary style. Maggie also put her professional librarian skills to good use to obtain the necessary permissions to publish many of the images.

Assisting Maggie were Judith Liebaert, Dara Fillmore, and Nancy Nelson. Judith and Nancy read and polished my manuscript, and Dara tracked down many of the images that I needed to tell the story. Working on this project apparently infected Dara with the maritime history bug, and she has now gone on to archive the massive collection of documents recently donated to the Jim Dan Hill Library at the University of Wisconsin–Superior by Fraser Shipbuilding Company, the successor to Alexander McDougall's American Steel Barge Company. I wish her well in this new endeavor.

This book was also enhanced by the work of two other individuals: the late Ken Thro and George Netzel. Ken Thro, tireless collector of Great Lakes documents, donated hundreds to Superior Public Museums. My ability to refer to these and to use them to illustrate the book contributed immeasurably to the finished project. George Netzel, a skilled draftsman, offered to prepare a set of drawings illustrating the numerous changes made to the whaleback steamship *Meteor*. While these are not included in the book, he also turned my rough sketch comparing whaleback vessels with conventional Great Lakes ships into the handsome drawing included in the book as plate 2, and I am grateful for his help.

I also wish to thank Professor Matthew Daley of Grand Valley State University. In the early stage of my research, Matt introduced me to some of the company's business records. The existence of these and others of a similar nature increased my ability to analyze the whaleback ships as an integrated part of a financial enterprise.

I was also helped by several institutions, namely the Jim Dan Hill Library at the University of Wisconsin–Superior, the Center for Archival Collections at Bowling Green State University, and the Mariners Museum at Newport News, Virginia.

Last but not least I would like to thank Susan Anderson, Superior Public Museums Executive Director (now retired), and Jim Sharrow, Director of Port Planning and Resiliency for the Duluth Seaway Port Authority. Eleven years ago, Susan and Jim got me interested in documenting the well-preserved steam machinery of the world's last surviving whaleback steamship, *Meteor*. One thing led to another, and this book is the result.

CHAPTER 1

The Life and Times of Alexander McDougall

T he whaleback ship reflected the experiences of her inventor, Captain Alexander McDougall, who decided in the 1880s that he could build improved, easily towed barges cheaply by using the relatively unskilled labor force available in his adopted hometown of Duluth, Minnesota. Captain McDougall's "dream" resulted in the construction of forty-three whaleback ships in the United States and inspired the construction of one whaleback steamship and over 170 "turret" ships of related design in Great Britain.

Alexander McDougall was a remarkable man. He was born in 1845 on the island of Islay off the west coast of Scotland. In 1854 he and his family immigrated to Canada, settling near Collingwood, Ontario, on Lake Huron. In 1861 he abandoned an apprenticeship with a local blacksmith, left home, and began a career on the Great Lakes as a deckhand aboard the steamer *Edith*. Aside from a night school course that he took during the winter of 1879–1880 in Buffalo, New York, McDougall's formal education ended at the seventh grade.[1]

From 1861 to 1880, McDougall "followed the lakes as deckhand, porter, second mate, mate, pilot, and captain."[2] During this time he met Thomas Wilson, a man who would have a profound influence on his later life. Wilson, also a Scottish immigrant, was captain of the freight and passenger steamship *Meteor* (not the same vessel as the whaleback SS *Meteor*). One author has claimed that McDougall was on board the steamer *Pewabic* in 1865 when she collided with the *Meteor*, resulting in heavy loss of life.[3] McDougall wrote in his autobiography that he was mate of the steamship *Iron City* for the entire 1865 season and then joined the *Meteor* as a mate in 1867, so if his memory is correct he would not have been present at the accident.[4] Both McDougall

A formal pose of Alexander McDougall, date unknown.
Source: Superior Public Museums

and Thomas Wilson would become successful in their own right, and Wilson's friendship would prove instrumental in McDougall's development of the whaleback ship.

In 1869 McDougall became a U.S. citizen, and in 1870 he was hired by the Anchor Line. In September of that year he was given command of their passenger and freight steamship *Japan*, one of three famous early iron passenger steamships operating on the lakes. This must have been a prestigious appointment for the twenty-five-year-

SS *Japan*, one of three identical iron passenger/package freight steamships launched for the Anchor Line in 1871. Alexander McDougall commanded this ship from 1871 through 1875. Source: UW-Superior Special Collections.

old Scottish immigrant. The Anchor Line was a major early Great Lakes steamship company founded by Edwin T. Evans with support from investors of the Pennsylvania Railroad. One of its major routes linked the Pennsylvania Railroad's western terminus at Buffalo, New York, with the Northern Pacific Railroad's eastern terminus at Duluth, Minnesota. The *Japan* sailed regularly from Buffalo to Duluth, and McDougall decided to build a house in this new city at the head of Lake Superior. He moved his mother and sister to Duluth in 1871, but until 1881 he spent much of his time while "on the beach" in Cleveland, Ohio, home to many Great Lakes ship owners.[5]

McDougall commanded the *Japan* for four seasons. During the winter of 1875 he was sent to Russia by E. T. Evans to look for opportunities in the Russian grain business. En route to Russia, he stopped at Liverpool, England, a port that would become important to him in later years.[6]

In 1879 he went to work for Thomas Wilson, who by this time managed his own

SS *Hiawatha,* a large (for its time) wooden steamship built by Thomas Wilson for the bulk cargo trades. McDougall supervised the construction of this vessel and its consort barge *Minnehaha* in Buffalo, New York. After their launch in August 1880, he commanded the *Hiawatha* for the remainder of the season. Source: UW-Superior Special Collections.

Great Lakes fleet. Wilson had ordered for his fleet two large wooden vessels: the steamer *Hiawatha* and the consort barge *Minnehaha.* After supervising their construction in Buffalo, McDougall commanded the *Hiawatha,* towing the *Minnehaha* during the 1880 shipping season.[7]

McDougall moved to Duluth in the spring of 1881. He built another house and, with the encouragement of Thomas Wilson, started what would become a successful stevedoring, marine insurance, and cargo business, but he was always thinking of new opportunities. In the early 1880s he decided to put his experience to work to design and build what he hoped would become a new, more efficient generation of lake barges.[8]

Fortunately for McDougall, the Great Lakes shipping industry was entering a period of explosive growth, and times were right for the introduction of newly designed

Alexander McDougall's first house, built in 1871 at 214 First Avenue West, Duluth, Minnesota. Source: Superior Public Museums.

ships. Unlike their British counterparts, who conservatively developed steamships from sailing ship hull forms, Great Lakes ship owners had already demonstrated an innovative spirit by designing specialized ships for Great Lakes commerce.[9] McDougall's invention of the whaleback ship would not, however, have occurred without the convergence of the following key factors.

1. By the early 1880s, the developing Great Lakes bulk cargo trades, mainly grain, coal, and iron ore, were generating a demand for new ships.
2. The federal government had agreed to fund and manage improvements to navigation on the Great Lakes, and work was underway to establish a channel capable of handling larger ships.
3. The technology existed to construct the new ships from iron and steel and propel them with steam engines.

4. An absence of restrictive regulations provided the opportunity for the invention and trial of radical new designs.

5. Capitalists with the funds to finance construction of these new ships considered the "Lake Country" to be a growth market.

By 1880, marine commerce on the Great Lakes, once dominated by small wooden sail and steamships, was poised for change. There was a need for efficient ships to haul the cargos that would feed America's industrial revolution. Great Lakes vessels hauled three types of cargo: passengers, package freight, and bulk materials. Lumber from the enormous pine forests of the north woods, used to build the cities of the Midwest, vied as the dominant cargo with grain, which was shipped in bulk from the prairie farms of Minnesota and the Dakotas down the lakes to Buffalo. Coal was an up-bound cargo, hauled from the eastern coalfields to cities around the Great Lakes. Coal was stowed as "paying ballast," but by 1880 specialized terminals to handle this cargo were being built in ports such as Duluth and Green Bay.[10]

Alexander McDougall would later attempt to build ships for both the passenger and package freight trades, but in 1880 he was interested in hauling bulk cargo, primarily grain and coal. Although McDougall's whaleback ship would eventually be intimately connected with the transport of iron ore, in 1880 this trade was still developing. The only active iron ore mines on the Great Lakes were those on the South Shore of Lake Superior working the Menominee and Marquette ranges. The ports handling this ore were Marquette, Escanaba, and St. Ignace, Michigan. The large ore deposits around the western end of the lake, including the famous Mesabi Range, would not be discovered and developed until the 1890s.[11]

Great Lakes commerce has always been constrained by depth of water in the various harbors and channels between the lakes, by falls at Sault Ste. Marie, Niagara Falls (between Lakes Erie and Ontario), and the rapids in the St. Lawrence River. Even after canals and locks were constructed around these obstacles, the size of the locks limited the size of the ships.

Prior to 1855, Lake Superior was isolated from the other lakes by the rapids in the St. Marys River at Sault Ste. Marie (known as the Soo Falls). Shippers wishing to transport cargos to or from Lake Superior were required to portage cargos around the falls and then reload them aboard another vessel. In spite of objections from political interests opposed to use of federal money to fund navigation improvements on the

Great Lakes, the State of Michigan was able to use money from the sale of federal lands to finance the construction of a canal and locks to bypass the falls.[12] Opened to navigation in 1855, the chambers of these locks were 350 ft. long by 70 ft. wide. In 1881 the new Wetzel locks paralleling the old locks were opened and the federal government assumed responsibility for the locks and connecting ship canal.[13] By 1881 the Soo Locks complex could handle any vessel launched during the whaleback era.

The obstacles created by Niagara Falls and the rapids in the St. Lawrence River were tackled by Canadian investors and the Canadian government. In 1829 the Welland Canal Company completed a canal bypassing Niagara Falls, with locks 110 ft. long by 22 ft. wide. By 1880 the Canadian government had improved the canal and enlarged the locks to 150 ft. long by 27 ft. wide. A year later another improvement by the government resulted in even larger locks with chambers of 270 ft. by 45 ft.[14] Although the whaleback ships are usually associated with commerce on the upper four lakes (Erie, Huron, Michigan, and Superior), the limitations of the Welland Canal lock chambers at Niagara Falls would still play an important role in the history of the American Steel Barge Company, which built the whalebacks.

Attempts to bypass the rapids in the St. Lawrence River began as early as the late 1600s. By the late 1700s, a canal with very small lock chambers had been built, capable of handling fur trade canoes and bateaux. By 1848 the canal had been widened, deepened to 9 ft., and fitted with locks 200 ft. long by 27 ft. wide. The canal would not be further improved until 1901, three years after the launch of the last whaleback vessel.[15]

The Civil War ended the domination of the southern agricultural interests that had opposed government financing of improvements to lake navigation, and funds became available from the U.S. Congress to deal with Great Lakes navigational hazards. In addition to harbor improvements, attempts were made to deepen the shipping channel. Although channel depth was not a problem that barred passage, it did restrict the amount of cargo that could be carried. The goal was to provide a channel 14 ft. deep on the four upper lakes: Superior, Huron, Michigan, and Erie. This involved deepening the locks at Sault Ste. Marie. By 1873 the state locks at the Soo had been deepened to 13 ft., and the new Wetzel lock opened in 1881 with a depth of 16 ft.[16]

The next obstacle to be dealt with was an area known as the "St. Clair Flats." The St. Clair River flows from the outlet of Lake Huron to the inlet of Lake St. Clair. At the inlet, the river forms a delta made up of several shifting and winding channels, restricting draft to 8 ft. and causing groundings. In 1855, before the Civil War, work began to dredge a channel through the Flats, but silt continued to restrict channel depth. In 1867, with federal funding available, work began again, this time to cut a canal through the area. The canal, with a low-water depth of 13 ft., was completed in 1871, but maintaining the channel in this area would require periodic work throughout the whaleback era.[17]

Shoals in the Detroit River provided another obstacle: one problem area was known as the "Lime Kiln Crossing," and the other area was located at the mouth of the river where it enters Lake Erie. With money from both the U.S. and Canadian governments, work to improve the channel through these areas would extend well into the next century.[18]

Great Lakes ship owners were quick to recognize the advantages of steam propulsion, beginning with the construction of the steamship *Ontario* in 1818. Early Great Lakes steamships were driven by paddle wheels, but in 1841 the screw-propeller-driven *Vandalia* was built at Oswego, New York. The engines driving her propellers were much smaller and lighter than the huge low-pressure, slow-speed engines used to drive paddle steamers. This allowed carriage of more cargo and elimination of the bulky paddle wheels that were a nuisance in the small lock chambers of the canals.

By the end of the Civil War there were fleets of "propellers" sailing the lakes, many operating as extensions of rail lines. Built to carry both passengers and freight, propellers often were built with boxy-shaped hulls to maximize space for carrying cargo through the small locks. A superstructure, usually two decks high, was built above the hull, running from the propulsion machinery in the stern to the pilothouse in the bow. This superstructure was pierced by large side ports called gangways for loading cargo. Cargo was stowed within the hull or on the main deck, protected from the weather by the superstructure. Passengers were accommodated in cabins arranged along the second deck above the cargo.

This arrangement worked well for packaged cargo that could be loaded and unloaded through the gangways but was impractical for anything shipped in bulk. Shippers with these cargos, therefore, continued to rely on sailing ships with their open decks. Eventually the advantages of steam propulsion became so compelling that some ship owners in the lumber trade built propellers without this interfering superstructure. Lumber could be loaded directly into the hull or stacked on the deck. These specialized craft with propulsion machinery aft and pilothouse perched on a raised forecastle forward were known as "steam barges."[19]

In 1869, the *R. J. Hackett* was launched at Cleveland. Built to haul bulk cargos of iron ore and grain, the *Hackett* was revolutionary. This vessel combined the steam barge arrangement of engines aft and pilothouse forward with the widest possible hatches spaced to match the spouts of the large gravity loading docks at Marquette, Michigan. While construction details evolved over time to adapt to new technology, including the change from wood to steel, Great Lakes bulk freighters for the next 100 years, including the *Hiawatha* that Alexander McDougall sailed, continued to be built on the *Hackett* model.[20]

Another early Great Lakes shipping practice copied from the lumber trade was the use of consorts. Because the size of individual ships was limited by a number of factors—channel width and depth, lock chamber dimensions, loading and unloading points located upstream on crooked rivers, and the wooden shipbuilding technology of the day—ship owners realized that the most practical way to increase cargo capacity was to tow one or more barges. These could be either schooners no longer sailing on their own or specially built barges. The old schooners used as barges were still rigged to sail, and Alexander McDougall once confided to an associate that the captains of these towed vessels often set sail in an ill-advised attempt to assist the towing ship. The *Hiawatha* towed the *Minnehaha*, a specially built consort barge.[21]

By 1880, therefore, the patterns of the Great Lakes bulk cargo trades were well established, with specially built wooden steam barges and towed consorts hauling lumber, grain, and iron ore down the lakes and coal on the up-bound journey. For Alexander McDougall to be successful, he would have to offer something that improved on this paradigm.

In 1843 British engineer Isambard Kingdom Brunel launched the steamship *Great Britain*, "the first vessel to embody all the elements of the modern ship in one hull: metal construction, steam driven screw propeller, and large size aimed at good economics."[22] During the 1880s this technology for building large engine-powered iron and steel ships spread from Great Britain to shipyards along the Great Lakes.

Iron hulled ships had occasionally been used on the Great Lakes since 1843 when the naval steamship USS *Michigan*, assembled from parts fabricated in Pittsburgh, Pennsylvania, was launched into Lake Erie. The first iron Great Lakes freighter designed and built specifically to haul bulk cargos was launched at Detroit in 1881, followed by the very successful *Oconto*, built at Cleveland in 1882.[23]

In the mid-1880s, steel, a stronger material, became commercially available in large enough quantities to be used for ships. The higher strength of steel permitted more cargo to be carried on a given displacement as less weight was required for hull structure.

Iron and steel construction also allowed the use of water ballast carried internally in watertight tanks. Water ballast could be quickly pumped overboard, eliminating delays associated with discharge of solid ballast materials.

The best high-strength shipbuilding material was useless without a practical method for producing strong, watertight joints. Fortunately, this problem had been studied in England for many years, where builders of early riveted iron ships were able to apply experience gained from the construction of riveted iron boilers to construct sound joints. Rivets were driven hot, and when allowed to cool they shrank to pull the surfaces of adjoining members together to form strong, rigid, watertight joints. This riveted construction required the development of industry standards that related rivet size, spacing, and pattern to the thickness of structural members being joined.[24] For example, the joint between two one-inch-thick plates joined by a double row of rivets is only 27% as strong as the plates being connected.[25]

Some sort of method to specify riveted joint design "good enough" for the service intended was, therefore, required as individual designers of hull structures could not be expected to have the time, expertise, or experimental data to apply basic structural engineering theory to the design of each riveted connection.

In 1859 in England, John Grantham published a book titled *Iron Shipbuilding* in which he advocated double riveting of hull seams and included drawings of riveting patterns. British mechanical engineer William Fairbairn published a paper in the first edition (1860) of the *Transactions of the Royal Institute of Naval Architects* that included a table titled, "Table exhibiting the best proportions for riveted joints."[26]

Meanwhile, Lloyds, the British classification society that had long published standards for wooden ships, had begun to write similar standards for vessels built from iron. The original standards issued in 1854 were overly conservative, but they were gradually refined over the years so that the issue published in 1885, which also included rules for building steel vessels, became the standard regulating the strength of British ships.

The first American standard for iron vessels was published by the American Shipmasters Association in 1872.[27] The preface of this document stated that they were largely compiled from the rules established by the Liverpool (England) Underwriters Registry and that this necessarily arose from the want of experience in America in

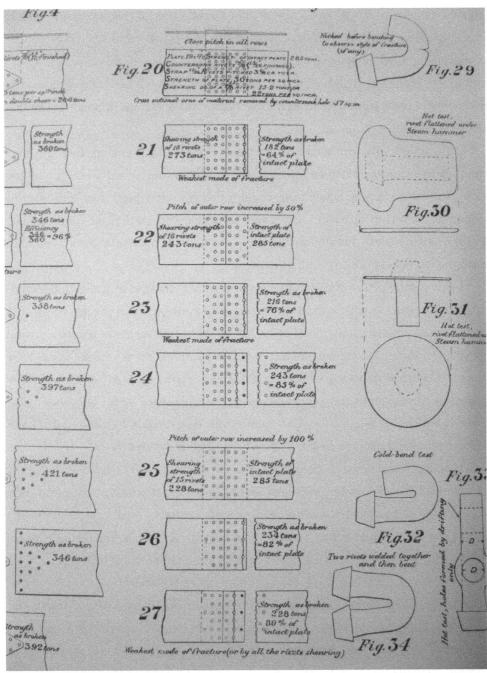

An example of standardized riveting patterns published in a nineteenth-century British shipbuilding text. Source: Holms Practical Shipbuilding, 1916.

iron shipbuilding.[28] By 1880, eight years after publication of this standard, a robust iron shipbuilding industry had developed on the East Coast of the United States, especially along the Delaware River, but much of the technology still came from Great Britain. To build his whaleback ships, Alexander McDougall needed technical help, and it would come from the Delaware River shipyards and from shipbuilders trained in Great Britain.

By the mid-1880s, technology for propulsion of Great Lakes ships had fully matured, using steam generated by high pressure Scotch marine boilers to power multiple expansion reciprocating, condensing engines driving screw propellers. This system of propulsion was so successful that it was not challenged on the lakes until the late 1930s, and ships using this propulsion system continued to operate on the Great Lakes until the last decade of the twentieth century.[29]

Unless constrained by the limitations of a particular trade or by navigation restrictions, ship owners usually utilized the largest ships available, as large ships cost less to operate than small ones per ton of cargo hauled. With the advent of riveted iron and (later) steel construction, shipbuilders could build much larger vessels. These were designed by naval architects who learned to think of ship hulls as huge box girders, loaded by the weight of the ship and its cargo, and supported by the buoyancy of the water in which they floated. This concept was fully developed in England by 1871 and allowed naval architects to design large, efficient hull structures.[30]

Shipping companies were usually collections of vessels with each vessel owned by local individuals who owned fractional shares. This allowed investors to spread their risk by purchasing a small interest in many vessels instead of owning a major interest in just one ship. While a fleet of ships would be managed by a "managing partner" or company that would paint all ships under its management with a distinctive color scheme, each vessel within the fleet might have different owners.[31]

When cash requirements exceeded the resources of local individuals, ventures could be financed by syndicates with access to capital. Often located in large East Coast metropolitan areas, syndicates arranged to borrow money from banks and sold shares in ventures to individuals they knew. One such investor was John D. Rockefeller who had enormous wealth to invest as a result of his ownership of the Standard Oil Company.[32]

An organization seeking to design a large ship today must satisfy a host of regulations issued by the U.S. Coast Guard covering issues such as freeboard, fire protection, lifesaving equipment, and pollution. Many of these issues are also covered by international treaty. In addition, classification societies around the world publish detailed standards for sizing the various structural members, for designing machinery, and equipping ships. Ships built to these standards (and inspected for compliance during construction) are then classified for insurance purposes. Without such a classification, vessels are difficult to insure. One such classification society is the famous British Lloyds Register of Shipping.

However, few of these regulations existed on the Great Lakes in the 1880s. The Steamboat Inspection Service existed to inspect boilers. Lloyds had published rules for building iron ships and maintained an office in Cleveland, Ohio. Of particular importance to the design of whaleback ships in the 1880s was the absence of load line specifications for Great Lakes ships to regulate the freeboard—the height of the ship's watertight deck above its waterline.[33]

In the absence of regulations, professional societies, and trained professionals, ship-builders relied on their own judgment, assisted by referring to textbooks published in Great Britain and to a few foreign-trained naval architects and marine engineers, usually English or Scottish and called "scientific men" by *Marine Review* magazine.[34] The scarcity of professionally trained engineers and the lack of formalized design requirements allowed untrained individuals to have influence over the design of ships that would be unheard of today.

By the early 1880s, conditions on the lakes were therefore favorable for McDou-gall's new venture. Great Lakes bulk cargo trades—grain, coal, and iron ore—were developing and generating a demand for new ships. The technology existed to con-struct these new ships from iron and later steel. The federal government had agreed to fund and manage improvements to navigation on the lakes, and work was proceeding to establish a channel with a minimum depth of 14 ft. capable of handling the new, larger ships. An absence of restrictive regulations, particularly freeboard standards, provided the opportunity for the invention and trial of a vessel of radical design. In addition, capitalists who had the funds to finance construction of these new ships and considered the "Lake Country" to be a growth market were available in the Lake Erie port cities and the major financial centers on the East Coast. The question was whether McDougall could convince these men to invest in his venture by producing a new seaworthy barge that would deliver cargo more efficiently than its conventionally designed competitors.

CHAPTER 2

Inventing the Whaleback Ship

Historically, ships have tended to evolve as conservative owners and builders slowly modified a few features at a time. Although the layout of deck structures on the early Great Lakes steam barge was new, these bulk cargo vessels utilized a hull form that had been seen before. Alexander McDougall, however, was confident that his experience on the lakes would allow him to build a superior vessel, and he set out to design a revolutionary barge, new from the ground up.

In his autobiography, written in 1922, McDougall provides a brief description of the barge that he believed would revolutionize marine commerce:

> While captain of the *Hiawatha*, towing the *Minnehaha* and *Goshawk* through the difficult and dangerous channels of our rivers, I thought of a plan to build an iron boat cheaper than wooden vessels. I first made plans and models for a boat with a flat bottom designed to carry the greatest cargo on the least water, with rounded top so that water could not stay on board; with a spoon shaped bow to best follow the line of strain with the least use of the rudder and with turrets on deck for passage into the interior of the hull.[1]

While McDougall does not elaborate further, it is possible to follow the evolution of his thoughts as he designed his barge by analyzing the three patents he applied for and received prior to the launch of his first vessel.

McDougall applied for the first patent in March 1880. The barge in this patent is a simple vessel with conical ends at both bow and stern. A cross-sectional view shows a cylindrical deck and cylindrical bilges merging into a narrow flat bottom making it almost elliptical in shape. A very small rudder was included that could be retracted

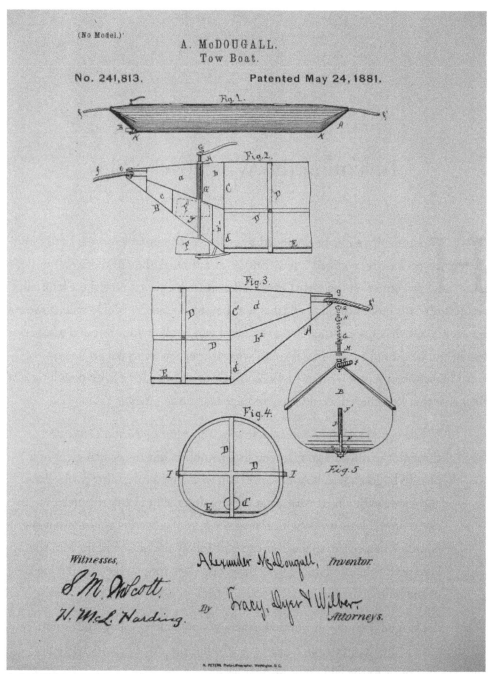

A drawing from U.S. Patent 241813, applied for by McDougall in March 1880 while he was supervising construction of *Hiawatha* and *Minnehaha*. This patent applies to a very simple, probably unmanned barge intended to be part of a train of similar vessels following the towing vessel.

into the hull structure when not needed. Tow lines were attached to the ends of the bow and stern. There were no living quarters for a crew because McDougall believed that the shape of the vessel's hull and its towing arrangements would allow it to follow the towing vessel without being steered. McDougall's initial concept was, therefore, a "train" of simple unmanned barges.[2]

Two years later, in April 1882, McDougall applied for and later received a second patent detailing a more elaborate vessel with the same cylindrical deck but with a much wider flat bottom. He added turrets at bow and stern to house equipment for handling an anchor and mooring lines. The stern turret included an elevated station for a helmsman, and the rudder was no longer retractable. McDougall had apparently decided that his barges would have to be manned by a crew that could steer. This patent describes a vessel that closely resembles his first barge launched in 1888. Had he raised the necessary financing in 1882, he could have launched his first whaleback six years earlier than he actually did.[3]

In April 1888, two months prior to the launch of his first barge, McDougall applied for a third patent. This patent further modified his whaleback design and added some features never found on any whaleback vessel. First, the cross section was modified to flatten the deck from its cylindrical shape to a semi-ellipsoidal one. This feature was duplicated on all whaleback barges and steamships that followed his first barge. Second, both bow and stern were reconfigured to a "wine glass" shape—a thin narrow fin that flared into a bulbous shape above. In the patent, he claimed that this shape would prevent the bow and stern from burying into waves and allow for the use of a more conventionally shaped rudder. While the modified stern bears some resemblance to the stern design of the whalebacks built after McDougall's first barge, no whaleback barge or steamship ever featured a bow as described by this patent. Two additional features never used in any whaleback vessel, barge, or steamship included sliding hatch covers sandwiched between the vessel's deck and a riveted guide and platforms set on multiple stanchions instead of single turrets.[4]

In this rather odd patent, McDougall states, "In building a tow boat of the character described, [he was then building his first whaleback barge] I have become aware of certain improvements over the inventions described in said Letters Patent, [his previous patents] which will better adapt the boat for carriage of oil, ores, coal, etc."[5] Who or what had caused McDougall to rethink his design in the middle of building his first whaleback barge?

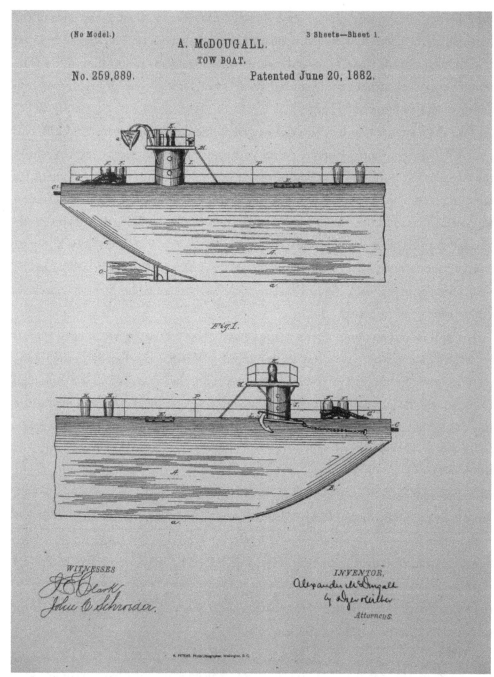

A drawing from U.S. Patent 259889, applied for by McDougall in April 1882. This drawing shows a vessel very similar to *Barge 101*, McDougall's first vessel. By this time, McDougall had apparently decided that his barges would have to be permanently manned by a crew able to steer them in the wake of the towing vessel.

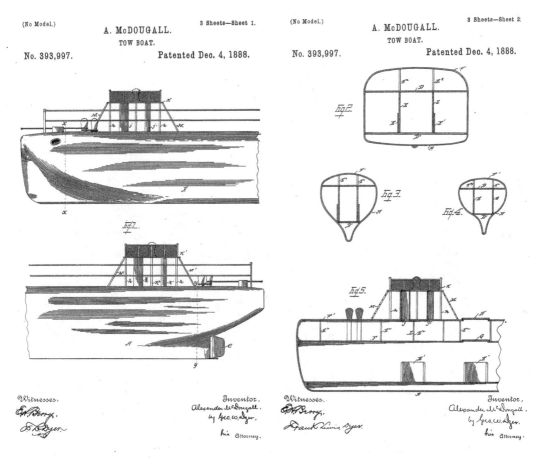

A drawing from U.S. Patent 393997, McDougall's third patent. Applied for in April 1888 during construction of *Barge 101*, the features included in this patent indicate that McDougall was hedging against the possibility that *Barge 101* would not be successful.

In the fall of 1887, McDougall had met a marine draftsman named Robert Clark. While he was not one of the new university-educated naval architects from Great Britain, Clark would prove to have a talent for modeling ship hulls. In this sense the term "modeling" refers to the art of determining the shape of a ship's hull, not building an actual scale model. Clark visited McDougall in Duluth to discuss future employment and later wrote that he reviewed the drawings for the barge that was being built. He wrote that he told McDougall the design was flawed in regard to the abrupt transition between the barge's parallel middlebody and conical stern, but it is possible that he had other criticisms and made additional suggestions as well.[6] Although McDougall refused to change his design at the time, he might have patented

A photograph dated August 1892 of Robert Clark with other American Steel Barge Company office personnel. Left to right, back row: Dan Brown, Frank Hayes, Mr. Starkweather. Front row: Hugh Calderwood, Robert Clark, Mr. Urquhart. Source: Superior Public Museums.

this modified design idea based on Clark's observations and suggestions—just in case his original design was found to be defective.

In 1888 McDougall decided to build a barge to demonstrate his ideas. The oft-repeated story that he built the barge without help from others is an exaggeration, as he used the typical scheme for financing Great Lakes vessels of selling shares to his friends. Owners of his first barge simply named *Barge 101* included McDougall, his friend Thomas Wilson, and business associates A. D. Thompson and Thomas Anthony.[7]

McDougall began by constructing a wooden scale model showing the shape of *Barge 101*'s hull. This was an old technique that McDougall would use many times when thinking about new ships to build. Trained naval architects had long been able to produce a set of "lines"—drawings in three views on a flat sheet of paper, describing the shape of a ship's hull—but before the advent of computerized drawing programs this was a tedious job requiring technical training, drafting skill, and some artistic ability.[8]

Although the hull shape for his barge was extremely simple and did not require the three-dimensional compound curves of later whalebacks, McDougall was not a trained marine draftsman or naval architect, so he carved this model to demonstrate his ideas. Author William Thiesen recently argued that the use of models to design ships reflects a sociological aspect of American shipwrights' attitudes to their work in comparison to their better-educated British counterparts, who relied on mathematical theories and plans.[9] This fails to consider that before the recent development of three-dimensional computer rendering, models were often the best way to visualize the complex shape of a ship's hull. With drawings, visualization is limited to the views presented on the drawing. A model, on the other hand, can be picked up, rotated, and touched with fingers that are quite able to detect areas of unfairness. Furthermore, many of the supposedly sophisticated British mathematical theories, such as the Scott Russell "Wave Line Theory," were later proven to be completely wrong.[10] Flow around a ship's hull is so complex that even today models towed in special tanks are used to evaluate hull designs and flow characteristics.

Further, the use of models to build ships was not limited to uneducated shipbuilders or to Americans. Yacht designer Nathanial Herreshoff, educated at the Massachusetts Institute of Technology and known as the Wizard of Bristol, used models exclusively

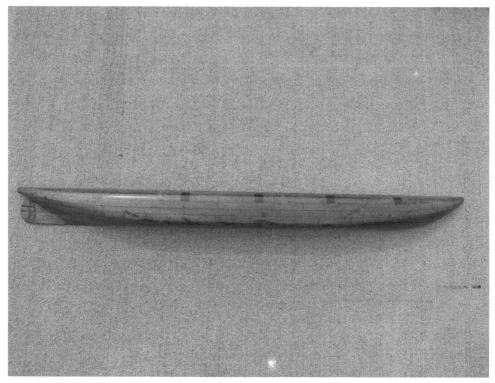

A half-model for the whaleback steamships *Washburn* and *Pillsbury* built in 1892. One of two such half-models known to exist (the other is for the whaleback passenger steamship *Christopher Columbus*), it is typical of the models built by shipbuilders to describe hull form and to illustrate plating arrangement. The four black rectangular marks along the hull mark the cargo gangways. Source: Superior Public Museums.

to shape his successful America's Cup defenders, and an English shipbuilding text printed as late as 1938 still included a chapter for making models.[11]

Like all Great Lakes ships, McDougall's barge featured a long (relative to the ends) parallel midbody section that McDougall believed he could build with his stevedore crews in Duluth. The conical ends at the bow and stern were another matter, so he decided to contract these to an experienced shipbuilder. With model in hand, he attempted to find someone willing to build them. After being rebuffed by yards on the Great Lakes, he traveled to Wilmington, Delaware, where the firm of Pusey & Jones agreed to build the ends of his barge. Robert Clark wrote that McDougall had "no details of construction or written specifications," so Pusey & Jones also apparently performed the detailed engineering to prepare working drawings from his model.[12]

These working drawings would have specified hull plating arrangement and thick-

A recent photograph of the location of McDougall's original Duluth shipyard.

ness; rivet sizes and riveting patterns; and sizing, spacing, and location of internal structural members for the entire barge. Two drawings for McDougall's barge, a plating plan and midship section, are known to exist.[13] The midship section plan also shows the timber blocking required to side-launch the vessel.

The one thing that McDougall did not lack was confidence. He supposedly said, "Nothing to it, only the nerve to tackle it." He was also critical of established shipbuilders for doing things in the same old way with "no improvements in their methods."[14] This criticism was unfair, for during the decade to come, shipbuilders along the lakes were to become famous for using advanced production techniques to achieve high productivity.[15] McDougall's outspoken opinions might have been one reason why Great Lakes shipbuilders refused to work with him.

Using his own labor force in Duluth to build the barge's parallel midbody and to reassemble the disassembled conical ends delivered by Pusey & Jones, McDougall was able to launch *Barge 101* on June 22, 1888, almost fifteen months after Pusey & Jones

McDougall's first vessel, *Barge 101*, being side-launched from McDougall's small Duluth shipyard. Side-launching was normal shipbuilding practice on the Great Lakes, and all succeeding whaleback barges and steamships built there would be launched in this manner. The vertical line extending into the water at the stern of the vessel is its rudderpost. The rudder has been swung over to starboard to avoid damage. Daylight can be seen in the triangular area between the rudderpost and hull, indicating the absence of a skeg (a vertical fin). Source: UW-Superior Special Collections.

prepared their drawings. This small, austere vessel was 137 ft. long by 25 ft. beam by 18.5 ft. in depth, with a gross register tonnage of 428 tons.[16] She closely conformed to McDougall's second patent with cylindrical deck, conical ends, and flat bottom. Pusey & Jones's working drawings indicate that she was transversely framed with heavy wood planks laid on top of open floors to provide a flat surface for carrying cargo. The bow and stern were identical, except that the stern was fitted with an open frame for hanging the rudder. If this frame was to be plated over to form a skeg, the drawing and a photograph taken during launch do not show it.[17] Two turrets were erected on the hull, one in the bow and one in the stern. A deckhouse was erected on top of the aft turret to provide shelter for the helmsman.

When speculating what McDougall might have hoped to achieve with his unorthodox design and how he expected its features to affect performance, there are several factors to consider: shape of the bow, buoyancy, hull openings, and cargo hauling capacity.

Great Lakes vessels of the time were designed with straight plumb, or nearly plumb bows. This feature increased what is known as the directional stability of the vessel (the tendency for it to proceed in a straight line). This is not always desirable in a vessel under tow as it prevents it from responding to course changes made by the vessel doing the towing. McDougall designed his barge with a conical-shaped bow to reduce its directional stability and allow it to more readily follow the towing vessel.

Also, the conventional straight bow can contribute to the vessel's tendency to "yaw" under tow. Yawing is defined as uncontrolled swinging back and forth, caused by uneven pressure build up on the two sides of the bow at the forefoot (the angled area between the horizontal keel and the nearly vertical stem). By eliminating this area where pressure builds up, McDougall's conical bow was intended to reduce yawing.[18]

As is often the case when designing a complex system, however, changing one feature adversely affects others. In this case, McDougall's conical bow would have made his barge easier to tow, but it would have reduced buoyancy forward and its ability to lift the ship over a wave, causing a potential major problem. In his classic work on steel shipbuilding, British author A. Campbell Holms states: "A vessel's wave riding qualities are greatly dependent on the fore-and-aft distribution of her reserve buoyancy; it is the bow and stern that first encounter advancing waves, and so, to lift promptly and avoid shipping water, it is here that buoyant power is most effective."[19]

McDougall's design also lacked sheer, adding to the problem. Sheer, the line of the deck on most vessels that sweeps up at the bow and the stern, not only improves the vessel's appearance but also raises the bow and stern higher above rough water. Eliminating sheer greatly simplified construction and reduced cost, but it further reduced reserve buoyancy at the ends and placed bow and stern closer to the water, allowing waves to sweep down the deck.

To compensate for this lack of reserve buoyancy in the vessel's ends, McDougall was forced to add a number of features that he later claimed as advantages.

Water trapped on deck by bulwarks or other structures would add unwanted topside weight to McDougall's ship, so he eliminated bulwarks and rounded the decks to shed water as quickly as possible. Further, ships of this period were typically built with graceful fan-shaped "counter" sterns, another feature that provided reserve buoyancy to lift the aft end of the ship when a wave passed under. This would have caused the spoon-shaped bow of a whaleback to pitch in a heavy sea, so McDougall designed his barge with a conical stern to reduce pitch by matching buoyancy in the bow.

Openings in a ship's hull were necessary to load and unload cargo. Until the 1920s ship hatches were commonly closed with heavy wooden boards set into raised structures, called coamings, which could be further protected in rough seas by tarpaulin coverings. On traditional ships, higher freeboard, sheer forward and aft, raised forecastles in the bows, and elevated decks in the stern to break the force of oncoming waves all served to protect these openings during rough weather.[20] Because whalebacks tended to plow into waves rather than to ride over them, McDougall instead designed small hatches, each closed with flush steel plates secured by dozens of stud bolts and sealed with rubber gaskets.[21]

Openings in the hull of a ship were also required to allow access below decks. Since McDougall's proposed whaleback barge did not have features to protect these openings from rough weather, he utilized steel doors for hull openings, placed in round steel towers called turrets. The turret in the stern was also used to support a pilothouse above the reach of expected wave heights.

All of these features were intended to improve towing performance and seaworthiness, but they did not contribute to the primary cargo hauling function of McDougall's barges, and in some cases they detracted from it. Conical ends reduced displacement that could have been used to float additional cargo, small hatches with bolted covers increased loading and unloading time, and rounded decks reduced internal volume that could have been used to stow light density cargo such as grain. If not to contribute to the money-making capability of the barge, why did McDougall persist with this design?

When he applied for his first patent in 1880, iron shipbuilding on the Great Lakes was still in its infancy. The first iron bulk carriers were over a year away, and no one could say for sure exactly how this new technology would evolve to produce successful ships in this era before the use of sophisticated economic modeling. At this time, new ship design was a blend of past practice and individual imagination. McDougall had as much right as anyone else to expect that his barge would be successful by "carrying the greatest cargo on the least water."[22]

To do this, he required that the barge feature a lightweight hull structure to maximize the percentage of the barge's displacement that would be devoted to hauling cargo. In addition, some of McDougall's ideas would simplify construction of his barges, resulting in reduced cost. Elimination of sheer saved weight and permitted duplication of transverse frames in the parallel midbody. Use of conical ends allowed

A stern view of *Barge 101* showing many of this first whaleback's unique features: a circular rounded deck, conical stern, and two tall turrets. Source: UW-Superior Special Collections.

elimination of heavy forged stem and stern posts and reduced the number of hull plates that required costly forming in two dimensions. By taking advantage of the inherent strength of the arch, curved deck framing could be made lighter and the heavy complex joint between side framing and deck framing could be eliminated.

One feature that did contribute to the whaleback ship's economic viability was its flat bottom. Newspaper reporters writing at the time and some authors since have described whalebacks as "cigar shaped ships."[23] While they may appear cigar-shaped in photos showing only the ship above the waterline, in reality the midship section of a whaleback is shaped like the capital letter *D* lying on its side with the straight side down. By providing maximum underwater volume, the flat bottom would provide maximum buoyancy to float heavy cargos through the shallow channels of the lakes.

By two accounts, *Barge 101*'s first trip was not successful. In 1893, a newspaper article published in the *Chicago Tribune* stated: "In 1888 Captain McDougall constructed the 101, a little vessel of over 1500 tons burden. He was then in Duluth. The 101 was regarded as a freak by vessel men, who christened it 'McDougall's Nightmare.' Soon after it was *towed into a rock and smashed*."[24]

Robert Clark, McDougall's associate, claimed that *Barge 101* yawed so wildly when towed that she had to be dry-docked in Cleveland for modifications. The barge's tendency to yaw probably accounts for the collision with the rock mentioned in the *Chicago Tribune*.[25]

What caused *Barge 101*'s erratic behavior? Robert Clark claimed that McDougall erred in making the vessel's conical stern too blunt. According to Clark, McDougall tried to save money by shortening the expensive conical section that he had to subcontract to Pusey & Jones.[26] If this is true it would have caused or contributed to *Barge 101*'s poor performance. Instead of flowing smoothly along the hull to the rudder, water would have separated from the hull in swirling eddies. Forces from these eddies would have contributed to yawing, and the eddies themselves would have impaired the rudder's effectiveness.

If the vessel was built without a skeg forward of the rudder, this would have also contributed to the problem. A skeg is a vertical fin mounted to the hull to direct the flow of water passing by. In this case, a skeg mounted to the bottom of the conical stern would direct flow into the rudder. Without a skeg the rudder would be operating in an area of confused water from the eddies being shed from the hull's conical stern.

Clark indicated that *Barge 101* was dry-docked in Cleveland to supposedly repair the damage to the hull and to increase the rudder size to improve steering.[27] The frame supporting the rudder could have been plated over at this time as well to form a skeg, as Clark shows a sketch of *Barge 101*'s stern with this area filled in. Whatever modifications were made, *Barge 101* apparently then operated well enough to be considered a success by the Cleveland vessel-owning community. In a December 5, 1888, letter to New York lawyer Charles Wetmore, Cleveland financier Joseph Colby wrote: "I don't think after seeing Captain McDougall you will need to consult any of your yachting friends. The performance of the boat already seems to satisfy everyone here that she is seaworthy."[28]

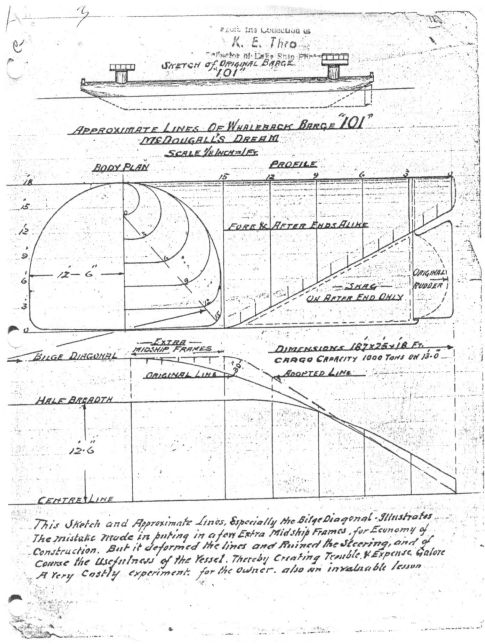

SKETCH OF ORIGINAL BARGE "101"

APPROXIMATE LINES OF WHALEBACK BARGE "101"

McDOUGALL'S DREAM

SCALE 1/8 INCH = 1 FT.

BODY PLAN   PROFILE

FORE & AFTER ENDS ALIKE

12 - 6"

SKEG
ON AFTER END ONLY

ORIGINAL RUDDER

BILGE DIAGONAL

EXTRA MIDSHIP FRAMES

DIMENSIONS 187 x 25 x 18 FT.
CARGO CAPACITY 1000 TONS ON 13-0

ORIGINAL LINE   ADOPTED LINE

HALF BREADTH

12·6

CENTRE LINE

This Sketch and Approximate Lines, Especially the Bilge Diagonal · Illustrates
The mistake made in putting in a few Extra Midship Frames, for Economy of
Construction. But it deformed the lines and Ruined the Steering, and of
Course the Usefulness of the Vessel. Thereby Creating Trouble & Expense Galore
A Very Costly experiment. for the Owner. also an invaluable lesson

A sketch made by Robert Clark, detailing initial problems with *Barge 101* and their corrections. This sketch does not resolve the issue of the skeg to direct flow to the rudder. Although the sketch shows a "skeg on the after end only," the word can have two meanings—either an open frame supporting the rudder or a plated-over fin. Source: UW-Superior Special Collections.

It took Alexander McDougall more than eight years from his original patent application to launch his first barge, a delay almost certainly caused by the need to accumulate the necessary capital to proceed. A positive development during that time was the growth of the iron ore trade as new mines were opened at the western end of Lake Superior. In the summer of 1883 the Minnesota Iron Company began shipping ore from Minnesota's first iron mine near Soudan out of the lake port of Two Harbors. The port of Ashland, Wisconsin, began shipping ore from the new Gogebic Range two years later. Overall, iron ore shipments from upper lake to lower lake ports increased during this decade from 1,908,745 tons to 7,292,644 tons. This tonnage did not include the huge ore deposits of Minnesota's Mesabi Range, which was not discovered until 1890.[29]

Unfortunately for McDougall, technology did not stand still during this decade. McDougall's autobiography states that he intended to build an iron boat; had he succeeded in doing so in 1880 it would have been the first iron lake freighter built for the bulk cargo trades. However, by 1888 Great Lakes yards had already been building iron vessels and were now building ships from steel, a stronger material that permitted the construction of larger vessels. McDougall's whalebacks would be built from steel as well, but his idea of building iron (or steel) hulled vessels to haul bulk cargo was no longer revolutionary.

The development of mechanized unloading equipment for the iron ore trade also occurred during the 1880s. Brown hoists and similar ship unloaders using self-closing clam shell buckets were built at Chicago and at ports along Lake Erie. Unlike the later Hewlitt unloaders with their clam shell buckets attached to a controllable rigid leg, the bucket on these unloaders hung from a less controllable cable, a particular disadvantage for the whalebacks with their small hatches.[30]

Ships in the bulk cargo trades also increased in size during this time. The 2,164 gross-ton *Oconto* launched at Cleveland, Ohio, in 1882 was already larger than any whaleback barge or steamship that Alexander McDougall would build prior to the steamship *Thomas Wilson*, his nineteenth vessel launched in 1892.[31]

Due to the rapid progress of both business and technology on the lakes during the decade, McDougall missed out on eight years that he could never regain. Meanwhile, Great Lakes vessel owners had discovered the economic advantage of operating fewer, larger ships instead of numerous small ones, a trend that culminated in the 1970s with the construction of today's "thousand footers." McDougall failed to accept this idea and continued to press for the construction of smaller vessels.

CHAPTER 3

The American Steel Barge Company

As the shipping season closed in late November 1888, Alexander McDougall's new barge proved successful; one whaleback researcher claimed that she completed nine trips during her first season.[1] Armed with this impressive performance, McDougall set about finding partners to finance the construction of more barges like *101*.

McDougall could have built his own fleet similar to the way that Thomas Wilson built his Wilson Transit Lines—one ship at a time, each ship financed separately through the sale of shares to the Great Lakes maritime, Cleveland, Ohio, and Duluth, Minnesota, business communities—but McDougall chose a different path. Though Wilson was an old friend of McDougall's, he apparently declined to buy whaleback barges for his Wilson Transit fleet; however, he did introduce McDougall to New York financier Colgate Hoyt. Wilson later bought shares in the resulting company.[2]

Colgate Hoyt was from Cleveland, Ohio. He was married to Lida Sherman, niece of Civil War general William T. Sherman and U.S. senator John Sherman, author of the Sherman Antitrust Act. Hoyt was an investment banker with the New York firm of J. B. Colgate & Company. He formed a syndicate with Charles Colby, a fellow member of the board of the Wisconsin Central Railroad, and Colby's brother Joseph, a lawyer.[3] This syndicate owned iron ore properties on Wisconsin's Gogebic Range and syndicate members realized that they would need a way to transport iron ore to the lower lakes from the Wisconsin Central's railhead at Ashland, Wisconsin. They were interested in McDougall's barges, and by late November 1888 McDougall was negotiating to sell them his barge design and barge-building equipment.[4]

The resulting contract establishing the American Steel Barge Company was signed on December 12, 1888. McDougall was to be paid $25,000 for his patents

Colgate Hoyt and his wife Lida Williams Sherman. Hoyt was a New York investment banker responsible for the financing of the American Steel Barge Company. He would be the company's president from its formation in late 1888 until its 1899 merger into the American Shipbuilding Company, although with much reduced influence following the events of 1893.

and $15,000 for his barge-building equipment. He was to work for the company for the next six months without compensation, other than dividends from his stock. He could purchase up to 20% of the initial stock in the company, and he had the right for investors that he nominated to purchase an additional 20%. This agreement applied to any future stock subscriptions as well. Had this scheme been carried out, McDougall and his allies would never have owned less than 40% of the company. If total stock subscriptions exceeded $200,000, McDougall would not have to pay for this additional stock with cash. The company would reserve these additional shares for him, provided he paid interest at the rate of 6%. This would presumably prevent dilution of McDougall's interest as additional capital was raised. The initial capitalization of the company, originally set at $100,000, was increased to "at least $250,000" in the resulting contract.[5]

Two subjects were not specifically discussed in the contract: purchase of *Barge 101* and rental of McDougall's shipyard. Records indicate that ownership of *Barge 101* passed to the newly formed American Barge Company in 1890, so McDougall and his partners presumably sold this vessel to the company for the approximately $40,000 it had cost them, as he had proposed to Charles Colby on December 4, 1888.[6] Why this barge sailed through the 1889 shipping season still under ownership of McDougall and his partners is unknown.

The issue of McDougall's shipyard was more complex and would ultimately become contentious. In 1884 McDougall had purchased a marshy strip of land along the waterfront of the harbor of Duluth. The property stretched along the present-day Railroad Street from Fifth Avenue West to Rice's Point (the site is known locally as the Superwood plant, which occupied the area from 1948 to 2012). He improved the property by pumping sand from the lake bottom using a dredge that he had built.[7] He used the area between Fifteenth Avenue West and Rice's Point to construct *Barge 101*. He continued to build additional whaleback vessels there until the company opened a new shipyard across the harbor in Superior, Wisconsin, in mid-1890.

Despite his lack of education, McDougall was a successful self-made businessman. By 1889 he was running several maritime-related businesses around the Duluth harbor that required an understanding of contracts, but the contract forming the American Steel Barge Company makes no mention of using McDougall's land. He later claimed to have unwittingly agreed to lease it in 1889 to the company for $1.00.[8] Documents also show that his partners in the company were anxious to get ships built, putting McDougall in a good bargaining position. It is, therefore, hard to understand how he could have been hoodwinked into agreeing to such a disadvantageous lease.

Further complicating the picture is a statement that McDougall made to Colgate Hoyt in a letter written in August 1889: "We have a lease of the property by paying the taxes."[9] He does not name the parties to the lease. Is it with him or an unknown third party? Another clue comes from McDougall's associate Robert Clark. In the handwritten draft of an article describing McDougall's invention of the whaleback ship, Clark included three photos of the American Steel Barge Company yard in 1889, with the caption: "The accompanying, marked I, II and III, show the yard as it was built in 1889 shortly after the American Steel Barge Co. was organized. Prior to this they and Plant was [*sic*] the property of Captain McDougall."[10] It therefore appears that McDougall agreed to lease his property to the new company in exchange for payment of the taxes, but as with other McDougall dealings with his partners in the American Steel Barge Company, use of his property remains a mystery.

The investment scheme for this initial capitalization is shown in table 1 and is of interest as it lists the names of individuals that would recur throughout the company's history.

Table 1: Initial Investors in the American Steel Barge Company			
Investor	Percent	Later Ownership	Relationship
A. McDougall	20	X	Inventor of whaleback ships
Thomas Wilson	5	X	Cleveland, Ohio, ship owner
C. W. Wetmore	5	X	New York lawyer
A. D. Thompson	5	X	Grain trader and McDougall friend from Duluth, Minnesota
Joseph L. Colby	5	X	Gogebic Range mine investor
Colgate Hoyt	5	X	Rockefeller associate
Charles L. Colby	5	X	Lawyer and Gogebic Range mine investor
Pickands Mather & Co.	5	X	Cleveland, Ohio, mine and ship manager
John. B. Trevor	15	X	Partner of James B. Colgate
James B. Colgate	15	X	New York stock broker
John D. Rockefeller	15	X	Owner of Standard Oil and investor
Francis C. Barlow		X	???? New York
Total	100		
Later ownership is based on an undated stockholders list in company records, Minnesota Historical Library, American Steel Barge Company records.			

The investors included in this table and the percentages subscribed are those listed by the partners when the capitalization of the company was anticipated at $100,000. It is not known if additional subscribers were added when capitalization was increased to over $250,000. When the company was incorporated on January 3, 1889, the articles of incorporation listed Colgate Hoyt, Charles L. Colby, James L. Colby, Charles Wetmore, E. B. Bartlett, George W. Weiffenbach, Robert D. Murray, Pickney F. Green, of New York, and Alexander McDougall as directors.[11] While McDougall, Hoyt, Colby, and Wetmore were all investors, the status of the others is unknown. It was the custom of the American Steel Barge Company to name its steamships after board members, and the only one of these "unknown" board members to be so honored was E. B. Bartlett who also appears later as an active board participant, providing reports on the administration of the business.[12]

Colgate Hoyt was elected president and treasurer of the new company, and Wetmore was elected vice president. McDougall was named general superintendent of construction.[13] This title does not reflect his actual role; today he would be the company's chief operating officer, responsible for designing and building ships while developing an organization and shipyard in Duluth, Minnesota.

The inclusion of John D. Rockefeller as an original shareholder is noteworthy. After making his fortune with the Standard Oil Company, Rockefeller invested in many ventures. His associate Frederick Gates later claimed that the ones sold to him by Colgate Hoyt were frauds, intended to "boom the towns" where the Hoyt syndicate had large real estate holdings. Rockefeller's biographer Ron Chernow echoed this claim. In his book *Titan*, Chernow tells of Colgate Hoyt selling investment schemes to an ailing Rockefeller while walking with him to church on Sunday. He further criticized Rockefeller for failing to properly analyze these schemes.[14] In the case of the American Steel Barge Company these criticisms ignore a number of important facts.

First, there is evidence that Rockefeller initially learned about McDougall's whalebacks from Thomas Wilson, not Colgate Hoyt. In his biography of Thomas Wilson, author Alexander Meakin writes: "When McDougall experienced difficulty in securing adequate financing for the development of his idea, Thomas Wilson spoke to his friend John D. Rockefeller in Cleveland about McDougall's idea. *Rockefeller suggested that McDougall contact his associate Colgate Hoyt in New York City* [Meakin's emphasis]."[15] If this is true, and Meakin claims that the statement is based on a note in the Wilson Transit Lines files, then Hoyt was checking out McDougall's idea on behalf of Rockefeller.

Second, when the company was formed, there was no assurance that the whaleback shipbuilders would purchase real estate owned by the Hoyt Syndicate in Superior, Wisconsin, to "boom the town" as Gates alleges. The first five whaleback barges and the first whaleback steamship built by the new company were built on McDougall's property in Duluth, and one year later, when it was decided to expand the yard, Mc-Dougall tried to buy additional property there before eventually moving to Superior.

Third, steel shipbuilding was "high technology" in 1889 and, as is often the case in such matters, no one knew what form ships built from this revolutionary new (to shipbuilding) high-strength material would finally take. History includes many cases of investors backing different competitive systems to solve the same technological problem; the Edison-Westinghouse debate concerning alternating versus. direct current power is just one example. It often takes a while for technology to evolve, and not all investors back the successful system.

In checking out McDougall's idea, the syndicate attempted to do what we would call today their due diligence. They discussed the performance of *Barge 101* with two experienced Great Lakes ship owners, Thomas Wilson and the firm of Pickands Mather. They researched McDougall's patents and hired a professional naval architect to comment on the whaleback design.[16] Since he did not own an established company, other than the records for *Barge 101*'s short single-season performance, McDougall would have had no financial results for them to review.

Either because his radical design was shunned by the conservative Great Lakes shipping community or because the project became too big to finance by selling fractional interests in individual vessels, or both, McDougall did what most inventors with high tech ideas do. He found venture capitalists to finance his idea in exchange for an interest in the resulting company. Initially, these venture capitalists would not have known whether McDougall's new ships would revolutionize Great Lakes shipping. Individually they could participate in McDougall's idea by each venturing what was a small investment for these very wealthy men. Unfortunately, in the years ahead the company's cash needs would grow to the point where the required investments were no longer small. But all of this was in the future. In January 1889, Alexander McDougall must have been a happy man.

CHAPTER 4

Early Whaleback Ships

In mid-January 1889, McDougall received approval from the American Steel Barge Company's board of directors to build a new, larger, whaleback barge, and he set about organizing a real shipyard on his Duluth waterfront site.[1] The resulting barge, which had almost three times the gross tonnage (a rough measure of internal volume) as *Barge 101*, would serve as the prototype for succeeding whaleback ships.

McDougall's problems with *Barge 101* must have convinced him that the very simple vessels envisioned in his early patents were not practical. For his new concept to work, he would have to refine *101*'s design, and to do this he would require professional help.

His first hire appears to have been Robert Clark, the man who initially described the problems with *Barge 101*. A letter written in 1896 and signed by McDougall says that Clark had been employed by the company since the spring of 1889.[2] An unattributed statement by a whaleback researcher says that Clark had worked as an apprentice at the Yarrow shipyards on the River Clyde in Scotland, a cradle of the British iron and steel shipbuilding industry.[3] Clark himself said that he first met McDougall while working at a shipyard in Buffalo, and his writings indicate that he first visited McDougall in Duluth in the fall of 1887 and was present during the construction of *Barge 101*. Although his title was chief draftsman, he functioned as a naval architect.

Also hired at this time was twenty-nine-year-old Hugh Calderwood. He had served a seven-year apprenticeship at Thompson's shipbuilding firm on the Wear River in northeast England. Mr. Calderwood was described as a draughtsman and loftsman, and while he would have assisted Robert Clark in preparing drawings, his title indicates that he had been trained to make full-sized patterns of hull structural members from scale drawings and other design information. Lofting was highly specialized work that McDougall had avoided to his peril when he built *Barge 101*.

The third man hired was forty-two-year-old Joseph Kidd. He had worked for English shipbuilders on the River Tyne and for John Roach, a leading American shipbuilder on the Delaware River. His skill seems to have been ship construction: translating drawings, patterns, and specifications into actual ships.[4]

By early February 1889 McDougall was looking for shipbuilding tools to buy. While we know that *Barge 101* was built under primitive conditions, we don't know what equipment McDougall did or didn't use to build his first craft. To build her efficiently, he would have required a plate shear, a punch, and a set of rolls for forming hull plating and structural members, all driven by belts from a steam engine. It is possible, however, that he didn't even have this equipment. He might have subcontracted bending of deck beams and bending of hull plates in the hull's straight section to someone else. He could have purchased hull plating sheared to size, and he could have drilled rather than punched rivet holes—not efficient, but practical with enough manpower. We don't know exactly what equipment he bought to build his new larger barge, but a newspaper report of the time stated that he installed "a large amount of machinery of the most massive description for bending, cutting, punching, and otherwise working steel plates and beams."[5]

We know that when McDougall built *Barge 101* he had no way to heat structural members for bending, so in the spring of 1889 he built a bending furnace.[6] Using this furnace, his shipwrights would have heated structural members red hot so they could be bent around pins set in holes on a perforated cast-iron table and arranged to match a pattern made in the mold loft. This technique allowed members to be bent to irregular shapes.[7] Without this technology and using only plate rolls he would have been limited to circular arcs, which may account for the circular contour of *Barge 101*'s deck. The hot bending equipment was housed in the center of the yard in an open-sided building that shows up prominently in old photographs.

One thing that he apparently did not invest in was improved material handling equipment. Material for *Barge 101* was moved about on carts and lifted into place with block and tackles using human or possibly animal muscle power. All succeeding vessels built in McDougall's Duluth yard were built this same way. Period photographs of McDougall's Duluth yard do not show even homemade stiff leg derricks.

Another labor intensive operation not mechanized was riveting. Although hydraulic and pneumatic riveting machines were becoming available, the company did not invest in this equipment until the late 1890s.[8]

While McDougall was shopping for equipment, Robert Clark was busy refining his original concept to produce a more practical vessel. Unlike the rectangular barges used today, consort barges used on the Great Lakes in the 1890s were unpowered ships, manned by small crews to handle tow lines, pump ballast and bilges, and steer the barge in the wake of the towing ship. McDougall had originally believed that his barges could be self-steering and unmanned. Operation of *Barge 101* proved this to be impractical, so Clark set about designing a more sophisticated vessel (see plate 1).

Clark provided a spoon-shaped bow to replace *Barge 101*'s conical one. These fuller bow lines increased displacement and buoyancy forward. *Barge 101*'s conical stern and skeg were replaced with a molded deadwood that flared into a long, tapered stern above and a heavy sternpost below. Concerned with *Barge 101*'s poor steering, Clark provided this fine-lined stern to ensure ample flow to the rudder.

Clark also flattened the new barge's deck, changing the circular shape to an ellipse. As the beam (width) of later whaleback barges and steamships increased, this elliptical shape would become flatter. Clark probably made this change to decrease the height of the ship under the ore dock, therefore increasing the slope of the loading spouts into the barge's hold.[9]

Another feature incorporated into the new barge's design was a doublebottom. Also called an innerbottom, or on the lakes, a water bottom. This was a watertight, framed, and enclosed space that extended athwartship (across the vessel from side to side) three to four feet above the vessel's bottom. Neither McDougall nor Clark invented this feature. It was first used on ships in the British coastal coal trades around 1860, and in the 1880s was beginning to be used on conventional Great Lakes ships as well.[10] Clark provided this doublebottom, not used on *Barge 101*, to protect the new barge in the event of a grounding; it was designed to remain afloat with a full cargo and flooded doublebottom. This new feature was also necessary to hold water ballast.

An empty ship will not handle well if it floats too high to get a grip on the water, or—in technical terms—to develop adequate directional stability. Ideally it should float to at least half of its design draft.[11] Great Lakes cargos were normally downbound from Lakes Superior and Michigan to Lake Erie. While it was possible to haul coal back up the lakes, this cargo was not always available and unloading of this cargo would delay turnaround at the upper lake ports. Barges and steamships returning

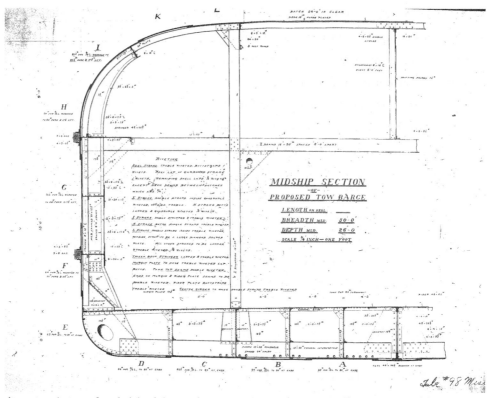

A sectional view of a whaleback barge showing its internal structure. Known as a midship section by naval architects, these drawings were and still are used in calculations to evaluate the strength of a vessel's hull. All subsequent whaleback ships were built with hull structure resembling that shown in this drawing, although longitudinal girders under the deck framing were included on the last five vessels built during and after 1896 to strengthen the hull. The imbalance between the heavy bottom structure and light deck structure is readily apparent. Source: Bowling Green State University Special Collections.

without a paying cargo would therefore have to be ballasted, and water carried in a vessel's doublebottom was the most convenient ballast material, as it could be rapidly loaded and discharged.

To assist the crew, the new barge was well-equipped with machinery powered with steam supplied by a boiler. Two steam pumps were provided for pumping ballast and bilges. A steam windlass and two steam capstans were housed in the turrets for handling the anchor and towing hawsers.[12] Some whaleback barges built later were fitted with steam-assisted steering gear, but this barge was steered by hand with a very large wooden steering wheel providing the necessary mechanical advantage.

Other whaleback features did not change. The new barge was provided with the same steel plate bolted hatches as *Barge 101*. Clark also retained *101*'s turrets fore and aft to provide access below and to house critical machinery. In addition, the new barge included a number of features patented by McDougall: special anchors, towing fairleads, and skylights made by sandwiching multiple small lenses between holes drilled in the vessel's steel plating and a second steel plate. While he was able to patent it, McDougall's skylight idea was an adaptation of an earlier concept that he modified for iron and steel ship construction. Circular lenses called decklights, used to transmit light below deck, have been recovered from wreckage of ships built on the lakes during the War of 1812.[13]

McDougall purchased the material for the new barge made-to-order from the Cleveland Rolling Mill Company, a steel distributor in Cleveland, Ohio. In an August 1889 letter to the American Steel Barge Company board, McDougall claimed that he lost approximately six weeks because of late material deliveries and that the mill slowed manufacture of his material "as they are interested [they own an interest] in the iron shipyards at Cleveland." To make up for the delay he paid extra to have the material shipped by rail instead of boat. He also incurred additional unplanned expense to incorporate unspecified changes recommended by several of the lake insurers.[14]

The resulting vessel, *Barge 102*, was launched from McDougall's Duluth shipyard on July 17, 1889, and was ready to sail ten days later on July 27. Henceforth, the American Steel Barge Company would name all whaleback barges sailing in their fleet with sequential numbers. *Barge 102* cost $67,500, which was $2,500 over the $65,000 not-to-exceed price authorized by the company's board—the apparent reason for McDougall's explanations to them.[15]

With an overall length of 260 ft., beam of 36 ft., and depth of 22 ft., *Barge 102* would fit into the locks of the Soo and Welland Canals but not the smaller locks in the St. Lawrence River.[16] Maximum capacity with a heavy cargo such as iron ore was 2,675 tons. Hauling this cargo, *Barge 102* would draw 15 ft. of water, leaving a freeboard of 7 ft.[17] As the cargo hauling ability of Great Lakes ships was often limited by fluctuating water level, the company in their economic calculations later assumed that these 260 ft. by 36 ft. by 22 ft. barges could carry an average ore cargo of 2,200 long tons per down-bound trip.[18.] Even after the American Steel Barge Company had added much larger vessels to its fleet, Alexander McDougall would continue to favor these "canal sized" barges.[19] For a comparison of *Barge 102* with a Great Lakes vessel of more conventional design, see plate 2.

Alexander McDougall was very pleased with the performance of *Barge 102*. In an August 14, 1889, letter to Colgate Hoyt, he wrote,

> In this first trip we learned that the *102* tows remarkably easy, the Captain of the *Sitka* (the towing vessel) and his Engineer as well as myself and the Captain of the *102* have come to the conclusion that she tows as easily as any 1500 ton vessel on our lakes and steers better than any large vessel we know of. It has been the custom on the lakes to pay one third of the gross freight from the tow barge to the motive power for towing round trip, but this has been mostly vessels of about 1,200 to 1,500 tons capacity. We started out to do this also, but I think in another season could do much better.[20]

Popular historical accounts of McDougall's whalebacks always seem to include at least one story of supposed experts ridiculing his design, but real experts seem to have taken Clark's improved whaleback barge design seriously.[21] In this same letter to Hoyt, McDougall reported that *102* and her drawings and specifications were examined by Captain J. J. Reardon, inspector for Lake Underwriters, and W. W. Bates, general manager for Inland Lloyds.[22] These inspections resulted in a rating for insurance purposes of A-1, the highest.[23] McDougall also patented this new design, the fourth patent he received for his whaleback barges.

Another, much later endorsement of the whaleback hull form was made by none other than the U.S. Navy. In 1960, as part of a project to investigate what they considered to be semi-submerged hull forms, the Navy's David Taylor Model Basin tested a scale model of the whaleback steamship *Frank Rockefeller*. While *Frank Rockefeller* was built several years after *Barge 102* and was probably designed by a different naval architect, the basic hull lines of the two vessels are similar. The Navy concluded, "The flow about this hull is considered very good within the speed range in which it was designed to operate. The flow around the bow is smooth, uninterrupted, and almost radial from the centerline. Flow studies indicate a dead water area just forward of where the propeller aperture would normally be (of course, *Barge 102* had no propeller), from about the 12-foot waterline to the water surface."[24] A good validation considering that McDougall and Clark did not have access to the Navy's extensive testing facilities.

By combining his ability to model ship hull forms with an ability to understand and apply up-to-date British iron and steel shipbuilding technology, Robert Clark transformed Alexander McDougall's concept as demonstrated by *Barge 101* into a successful and practical vessel. Clark's design was so successful that it would be used in a variety of different sizes for nearly all succeeding whaleback barges and steamships. However, Clark's improvements came at a price. These succeeding whalebacks would be more complex and difficult to build, changing the whaleback ship from McDougall's idea of simple, cheap vessels that could be built by unskilled labor.

On April 1, 1889, McDougall was authorized to build another barge, a duplicate of *102*. *Barge 103* was launched on October 5, 1889, and her construction reflected the yard's growing expertise as she cost $5,800 less than her earlier sister. Barge building at the Duluth yard continued with the launch of three lengthened sisters of the *102* design. With an overall length of 284 ft., these were designed exclusively for trading on the upper Great Lakes as they were too long to fit into the Welland Canal locks. The last of these, *Barge 107*, was launched on August 16, 1890, and was the final vessel to be built at the Duluth yard.[25]

While these five barges were being built in Duluth, two more were under construction by the firm of Hendren & Robins at Brooklyn, New York. Launched on the same day in April 1890, these two barges, named *Barge 201* and *Barge 202*, were designed to fit into the small lock chambers of the St. Lawrence River at Montréal.[26] Construction of these two small whaleback barges was probably contracted out to the Brooklyn firm because McDougall's small Duluth ship yard did not have the capacity to add two more vessels to its workload, and McDougall and his investors were anxious to place ships of whaleback design into saltwater commerce.

From its beginning, the company anticipated building steam-powered vessels to tow its barges. Construction of "steam tow boats" is mentioned in McDougall's contract, and a lack of steamships owned by the company required them to pay one-third of the towed barge's revenue to others (usually Thomas Wilson) for towing charges.[27] On February 5, 1889, McDougall wrote to Wetmore that he was looking for tugs, presumably to purchase or charter, that could tow the company's barges.[28] This was six months prior to the completion of *Barge 102*.

In the event, no tugs were purchased, and on June 9, 1890, the American Steel Barge Company launched hull 106, its first steamship, the 287 ft. long by 36 ft. wide by 22 ft. deep 1,253 gross ton *Colgate Hoyt*.[29] Like all other whaleback steamships built for the bulk cargo trades, this vessel was capable of both carrying cargo and towing barges. As with his barges, the design of the steamships was patented. This patent,

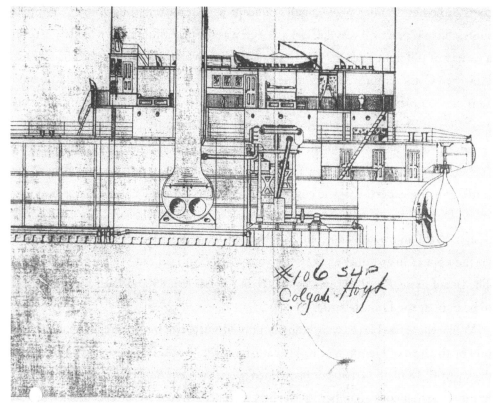

A section of the inboard profile drawing of the first whaleback steamship *Colgate Hoyt* showing the aft end of the ship with its propulsion machinery. The reciprocating steam engine is a compound—steam expanded in two stages and the engine is tall enough to protrude through the top of the hull into a turret built overhead. The athwartship arrangement of the boiler is curious and was not repeated in subsequent ships. In later ships the compound engine would be replaced with triple expansion ones and the orientation of the boiler changed to longitudinal. Otherwise this basic design would be used for all succeeding whaleback steamships built on the Great Lakes prior to 1896. Source: Bowling Green State University Special Collections.

number 429,468, was granted to McDougall on June 3, 1890. McDougall claimed that he was patenting "a steam tow-boat especially adapted for towing other vessels and for carrying freight."[30]

Robert Clark modeled the *Colgate Hoyt* by modifying the *Barge 102* hull form to add a propeller aperture. The fore-body and midship section did not change.[31] The new vessel was also provided with a redesigned rudder. The barges all featured a rudder hinged to the vessel's sternpost. The *Colgate Hoyt* used an elliptical-shaped "balanced" rudder pivoting about a shaft that passed through its center to a bearing housed in a strut protruding from the hull. Balanced rudders were not new. They had been used on Civil War monitors, but McDougall was able to obtain a separate patent for this design.

While these rudders were satisfactory in a fresh water environment, one feature claimed by his rudder patent supposedly caused the grounding of the whaleback steamship *Charles W. Wetmore* when she was sailing in salt water. The rudder was built by filling a steel frame with oak planking, the whole thing plated over on both sides. McDougall claimed that water leaking in past the plating would cause the wood lining to swell tightly within the frame, but *Marine Review* reported that acid from the oaken lining in conjunction with seawater corroded the steel frame causing the rudder to fail.[32]

As with most other propeller-driven Great Lakes ships, the *Hoyt*'s machinery was located as far aft as possible, providing clear decks for handling bulk cargos but causing the ships to trim heavily by the stern when light. Instead of two turrets, one forward and one aft, there were now four: one forward and three aft. The aft turrets included one for access below, one to house the boiler uptake, and one over the engine. Early American-built steam engines were quite tall, and the cylinders of the *Hoyt*'s engine protruded into this turret. The short pilothouse of the barge was extended to become a deckhouse spanning the three aft platforms. The pilothouse was located on top of the deckhouse. Although the preferred location for pilothouses on Great Lakes vessels was in the bow, the whalebacks' tendency to plow through waves would have made this location impractical.

We do not know who designed the *Hoyt*'s steam machinery. The 755 hp compound engine (steam expanding sequentially in two cylinders) was built by S. F. Hodge, one of two Detroit engine manufacturers. Steam was supplied by two Scotch marine boilers built by Lake Erie Boiler Works of Buffalo, New York. Steam pressure was 120 psi (pounds per square inch).[33] Steam from the low pressure engine cylinder exhausted to a condenser. This steam plant supplied plenty of power as the *Hoyt* reputedly could steam at 16 mph, quite fast for a Great Lakes bulk carrier of the time.[34] Without sophisticated model testing capabilities, the American Steel Barge Company's engineering department may have misjudged the size of the power plant required to propel the easily driven whaleback hull, or they may have felt that it needed this extra power to tow the large whaleback barges. In either case, before the days of radio dispatching, an extra burst of speed could come in handy as the first vessel to reach the ore docks was the first to be loaded.[35]

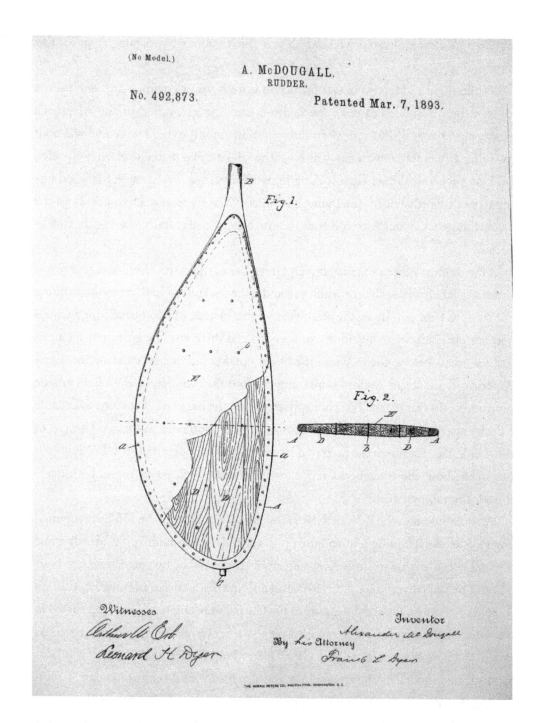

A. McDOUGALL.
RUDDER.

No. 492,873.

Patented Mar. 7, 1893.

Fig. 1.

Fig. 2.

Witnesses
Arthur A. Orb
Leonard H. Dyer

Inventor
Alexander McDougall
By his Attorney
Frank L. Dyer

A drawing from U.S. Patent 492873, McDougall's patented rudder, which was known as a balanced rudder because forces acting on the area forward of the rudderpost would partially balance those acting on the area aft of it. The steel frame, wood lining, and steel plating are all clearly shown.

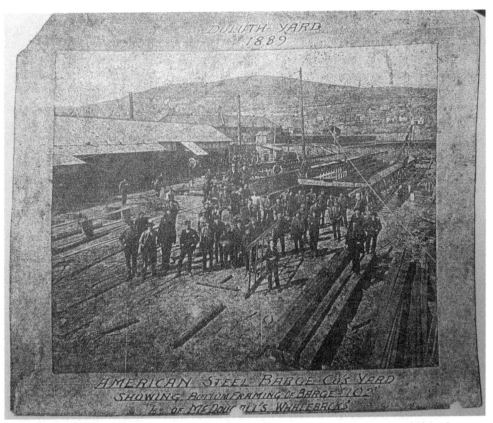

A photograph of McDougall's original small Duluth shipyard where the first six whaleback barges and the first whaleback steamship were built. The slip into which the vessels were side-launched was located just to the right of the photo. Source: Clark, "Genesis of the Whaleback Ship," UW-Superior Special Collections, Ken Thro Collection.

The *Colgate Hoyt* was considered a success and served as the prototype for succeeding whaleback steamships. With a gross register tonnage of only 1,253 tons, she could load 2,491 long tons of a heavy cargo while drawing 15 ft. of water. The ratio of cargo capacity to gross register tonnage, a measure of her cargo hauling efficiency, was 1.988, which was considered good for vessels in the Great Lakes bulk cargo trades, and her easily driven hull form would have reduced coal consumption.[36]

On February 8, 1890, the *Duluth Daily News* reported:

At 3 o'clock this afternoon the Zenith City is to witness the first midwinter launch. At that hour Captain McDougall will give the word to let the *104* slide into the water. All day yesterday 150 men and 20 teams were busily engaged in cutting the ice in order to afford an opening into which the vessel might glide. The *104* is the largest carrier on the lakes, achieving a capacity of over 2900 tons on a draft of over 15 feet. Her length is 284 feet, beam 36 and hold 22. The shipyard now employs 400 men. Work is progressing on four boats, the *101* which is being remodeled at the ends, *104*, *105*, and *106*. The last mentioned is to be the first of the steel steamers to be manufactured by the American Steel Barge Company. Her frame is now being bent. Work will commence on the *107*.[37]

The statement regarding the modification of *Barge 101* is noteworthy. Apparently Robert Clark's modifications to McDougall's whaleback concept design were effective enough to warrant extensive modification of this small vessel.

The claim that *Barges 104, 105*, and *107* were the largest carriers on the lakes is not correct. These barges, with a gross register tonnage of 1,295, were considerably smaller than the iron steamer *Onoko*, built in 1882 and registered at 2,164 gross tons, or the ill-fated early steel steamer *Western Reserve*, built the same year as the barges and registered at 2,392 gross tons.[38] The *Onoko* could haul 3,073 tons of ore, compared to 2,656 tons of the same cargo for the barges.[39]

It's safe to say that by 1890 McDougall's small Duluth shipyard was buzzing with activity, and, quibbling aside, in the short fourteen months since its inception, the American Steel Barge Company had mastered the technology to build efficient (for 1890) steel-hulled vessels that were competitive in Great Lakes bulk trades.

CHAPTER 5

The New Shipyard

As the year 1889 drew to a close, Alexander McDougall should have been proud of all he had accomplished. The company had built two barges and was working on three more barges and one steamship that would be launched during the coming year.[1] By that time the American Steel Barge Company would be operating a sizable fleet of modern efficient vessels that would move 125,966 tons of ore during the 1890 shipping season.[2] The company could have focused its attention on improving the management of these ships while continuing to operate the Duluth yard as a facility for constructing new vessels as market conditions required and for maintaining its existing fleet. By building even one or two additional steamships the company could have eliminated the expense of having others tow its barges.

Instead, they embarked on a more risky course of action. No production manager ever has enough room or a large enough facility to get his job done, and McDougall and Clark were no exception.[3] Both complained of cramped and wet working conditions despite the fact that the Duluth yard would be adequate to launch three barges and a steamship in the first eight months of 1890. In his autobiography, McDougall claims that his original intent was to acquire additional property adjacent to his yard to provide more space, but he was discouraged from doing so by members of the Duluth business community, who did not want a noisy, dirty shipyard close to the downtown business district.[4] After investigating property in West Duluth, McDougall decided to accept an offer from R. J. Wemyss, general manager of the Land and River Improvement Company, to locate a new shipyard across the St. Louis River in the new community of Superior, Wisconsin, only a mile or two from the old one in Duluth.[5] Like many business deals today, this offer came with a significant financial incentive;

The very large vessel assembly shed at the new West Superior shipyard with a barge ready for launch in the foreground. This barge would have been assembled out of the weather from steel structural shapes and plate prefabricated in the company's shops. The assembled vessel would then have been moved out of the building to the position shown on the photo for side-launching into the adjacent slip. Source: Superior Public Museums.

the Land and River Improvement Company would subsidize the shipyard's payroll by 10% for a savings over time of $200,000.[6]

After accepting this offer, the company began construction in February 1890, and the yard was ready in time to build *Barge 109* and the steamship *Joseph Colby*, both launched late that year. Building this new shipyard was a huge undertaking requiring dredging of the bay and filling of wetlands along the waterfront. Five finger piers were dredged from the bay to provide building ways for eight ships. A huge steel building was erected on one pier to permit two ships to be assembled inside during winter weather. This building was fitted with detachable sides to allow the completed hulls to be moved outside for launch.[7] Later photographs also show multiple hulls being built outside surrounded by multilevel wooden scaffolding. One photograph shows a sheer-leg-type crane for lifting heavy equipment, but there is no evidence that jib, gantry, or overhead cranes were installed in 1890 for handling shipyard materials.

Yard facilities included a 180 ft. by 40 ft. carpenter shop, a 100 ft. by 201 ft. machine shop, a 70 ft. by 170 ft. blacksmith shop, a 40 ft. by 90 ft. two-story office/warehouse building and a 25 ft. by 40 ft. brick boiler/engine house.[8] The carpenter shop would have been used to make wooden patterns for fabricating steel parts such as the curved hull frames. The shape of these patterns would have been lifted from a full-sized layout of the ship's hull marked on the mold loft floor—a large flat wooden floor that might have also been located in the carpenter shop or the office. It was not necessary for the floor to be as long as the ship, as a skilled loftsman could fold the hull shape back on itself on the floor. The carpenter shop would have also held the woodworking tools required to mill lumber for wooden deck structures erected on top of the turrets.

The blacksmith shop would have housed machinery for hot working steel. The heart of this activity would have been a furnace for heating steel to be bent or forged. This building would have also housed the large cast-iron platens upon which steel shapes were bent, a steam-powered forging hammer, and tools for forging smaller shapes by hand.[9] The machine shop carried out other metalworking activities. Its equipment included a pipe machine, steam-powered rolls for bending plate and structural shapes, three planers for milling the edges of plates, four countersinks for countersinking rivet holes, two angle iron cutters, two horizontal punches, six combined vertical punches and shears, a bolt machine for threading, and metal cutting lathes.[10] The pipe machine probably flared pipe ends to accept loose flanges for bolting sections together, as the technology for welding piping sections together was not yet developed. For its day, the yard was considered to be well-equipped.[11]

All of this equipment required some sort of motive power. Some equipment, such as the forging hammer, was powered by direct application of steam routed through the yard by pipes running from the boiler house. Other equipment was powered by flat belts driven by a system of rotating shafts that would have passed through the yard. Turning this shafting was a 75 hp steam engine located in the boiler house.[12]

Steel for the first barges was purchased from mills in Cleveland and shipped up the lake by steamer. Beginning with the steamship *Washburn*, launched in June 1892, iron and steel materials were purchased locally from the West Superior Iron and Steel Company, another Hoyt Syndicate enterprise.[13] This material would have been riveted together. Driven hot, these rivets would shrink upon cooling, pulling the joint firmly together. A ship the size of a whaleback could require hundreds of thousands of rivets, and the labor to drive them could consume 35–40% of labor costs.[14] In 1890 each rivet was driven by hand by a three- or four-man crew. Author A. M. Rob describes the process:

#107 & 108

An American Steel Barge Company shipyard gang in front of a vessel under construction. The wooden strips are patterns made in the yard's mould loft from full-sized drawings of the ship scribed on the loft's floor. Source: Superior Public Museums.

> The rivet is heated in a portable fire-hearth blown by bellows and passed—sometimes thrown—by the rivet heating boy to the holder-on. The holder-on knocks the rivet through the hole and holds it in place with a heavy hammer; the head of the rivet is commonly of "pan" shape. . . .
> The point of the rivet—the end of the parallel shank projecting from the head—is hammered up by two riveters striking alternatively, if the rivet is to fill a countersink.[15]

This system of driving rivets by hand was used to build nearly all of the whaleback ships. Pneumatic and hydraulic riveters were not introduced at the yard until its modernization in 1897, just prior to construction of the last whaleback ship, the steamship *Alexander McDougall*.[16]

Unlike many other shipyards of the time, American Steel Barge did not build engines or boilers. These were bought from other companies. Of the sixteen whaleback steamships built by the American Steel Barge Company, eleven used engines built by the S. F. Hodge Company or by Frontier Iron Works, both of Detroit, Michigan. Frontier was started by employees from Hodge. One engine was bought from the Doxford Yard in England to evaluate English engine building practice. The results of the test were apparently not convincing, as no more English engines were bought.[17]

Managing this modern, well-equipped shipyard, high-tech for the times, was a team of men educated in the field of iron and steel shipbuilding. While Robert Clark, Hugh Calderwood, and Joseph Kidd have already been introduced, a report written by Charles Wetmore, the company's second vice president, provides information about the rest of these key people.[18]

> *William Mahon*: Mahon, age twenty-three, was responsible for design of the machinery for the barges and steamships. He was educated at the Boston School of Technology, had been chief draftsman at the Frontier Iron Works in Detroit, and had also worked at a new machine shop in Duluth. He had a total of six years of experience. He would have finished his education and started work at age seventeen.
>
> *A. C. Diericx*: Deriux was a naval architect who had been recommended by William Johnson, an English ship owner friend of McDougall's. Diericx had served seven years at Woolwich, a Royal Navy dockyard, and as chief draftsman for Rouden at Liverpool. Wetmore commented, "Apparently very able as a mathematician and calculating and in preparing specifications—I think this will fill a want that we have had ever since the beginning."[19] The calculations that Wetmore refers to are called form calculations. These predict such characteristics as displacement, trim, and lateral stability. Deriux would also have been responsible for the structural design of the vessels; his signature appears on many of the drawings for whaleback ships. Deriux must have been highly regarded; he would survive the 1900 merger of the Great Lakes shipbuilding industry to become head of the hull department for the newly merged American Shipbuilding Company.
>
> *Frank Hayes*: Hayes, educated at the Stevens Institute of Technology, was employed for one year in machinery, hull construction, and design. It was noted by Wetmore that Hayes was the "only son of a wealthy Superior family."[20]
>
> *Charles Wachtel*: Wachtel served as cashier.

Captain Ira Harris: Captain Harris was auditor and in charge of the material department.

Joseph Crawford: Crawford, fifty years of age, was material agent (would be called a purchasing agent today) and bookkeeper.

Robert Clark left the company in the fall of 1892, before Wetmore's report was written, therefore he was not mentioned. The opinionated Clark must have clashed frequently with the equally opinionated McDougall, but the two apparently had a relationship of mutual respect, as Clark's granddaughter claims that he assisted in the preparation of McDougall's autobiography in the 1920s and was hurt that McDougall did not acknowledge it. Clark would end his career working for the federal government on the West Coast.[21]

Charles Wetmore ended his report by stating, "The rest of our office help are young men, some of them have a great deal of promise for the interest of our company." In addition to the management team, employment at the yard had grown to 2,000 by the end of 1891.[22]

On Christmas day of 1891, the company broke ground for a drydock. Excavated with horse-drawn scoops, the 537 ft. long dock was receiving ships by late summer/early fall and would eventually prove to be the yard's most valuable asset.[23]

The yard was modernized in 1897. A large gantry crane serving several shipbuilding berths was constructed, in addition to the previously mentioned improved riveting machinery. Period photographs show this crane lifting hull plates used to build the whaleback steamship *Alexander McDougall*. This modernization also brought electrification to the yard. A 150 kW steam-driven generator supplied electric power to a yard lighting system and to electric motors driving machine shop equipment. Plans were also put in place to construct a second smaller drydock and to build marine steam engines, but these plans were not executed during the whaleback era.[24]

Although physically impressive, the new yard made little financial sense for a number of reasons:

1. In 1889 there was no evidence that other ship owners would adopt the whaleback design and become American Steel Barge customers; in fact, they never did.
2. To keep the yard busy, ships would have to be built whether they were needed or not. In the absence of outside customers, these newly built vessels

The office force of the American Steel Barge Company. McDougall is seated third from the left. Immediately to his left is A. C. Diericx, the company's naval architect. Source: UW-Superior Special Collections.

would have to be added to the company's fleet. This ever-expanding fleet of whaleback barges and steamships would require ever-increasing amounts of capital. In the winter of 1890–1891, for example, the company increased its capitalization from $2,000,000 to $5,000,000 by selling stock.[25]

3. Correspondence between members of the Hoyt Syndicate (particularly McDougall) about increasing demand for shipping in the "Lake Country" were not supported by rising freight rates.[26] As table 3 in chapter 6 illustrates, contract rates for shipping ore from Lake Superior to Lake Erie ports were trending downward at the time.

4. The company's most urgent business problem was operating its vessels efficiently, not building new ones. Increasing the number of trips per season for ships in the fleet, what McDougall called the "dispatch," was a more efficient way of increasing the annual carrying capacity of the fleet than building new ships.

5. If working conditions in the original Duluth yard were as primitive as

reported, one would think that labor costs would fall in the new more-efficient yard. Such was not the case. McDougall faithfully recorded the costs for building each barge and steamship in a personal account book. In this book, wages for each vessel are listed separately. Labor costs per light ship ton or gross register ton were both found to be over 10% higher for barges built in the new yard than those built in the old Duluth yard.[27]

Considering all of these factors, it is hard to understand why intelligent, experienced investors found it necessary to invest in a new shipyard. They might have been carried away by the buoyant optimism of the day. For example, in late 1892 or early 1893 the city statistician of Superior wrote in his annual report:

> The American Steel Barge Works were established in the early part of 1890 and, in that year, completed several boats and laid the keel of others. Such has been the triumphant progress of the enterprise that up to the present there have been constructed nine steamers and twenty barges. The success of the whaleback pattern of vessels in economy of construction, in carrying capacity, and in speed and safety, has been abundantly demonstrated that in the past year some of the shrewdest and wealthiest business men in the United States have put $1,000,000 of additional capital in the enterprise. The proprietors of the barge works now own controlling interests in the Mesaba iron mines where the raw material is procured, in the railroad by which it is transported to the blast furnace[,] in the rolling mills in which it is converted into plates and other structural forms and, and finally in the largest and most complete shipyard on the great lakes, constituting a stupendous combination of inexhaustible resources and independent means of production equaled nowhere else in the world.
>
> During the year 1893 the company expects to launch sixteen new vessels or one every three weeks.
>
> Here was erected that marvel of transportation, the passenger steamer *Christopher Columbus*, having a carrying capacity of 5,000 people and making an average speed of twenty four miles an hour.
>
> In 1892 the same company built an immense drydock, the largest on the Great Lakes, and the only one on the upper lakes. It is 550 ft. in length, 90 ft. wide at the water level, and 52 ft. wide at the bottom. During the winter

it stored for repair one whaleback steamer, one whaleback barge and five lake tugs. Its constant use shows its importance to the vessel interests, and during 1893 another dock of practically the same dimensions but deeper will be constructed by its side. It is now no longer necessary to send vessels large or small on long and expensive trips to the lower lake ports for repairs. Thus thousands of dollars and much valuable time will be saved to vessel men and the city is enriched by the great earning capacity of the plant.[28]

But perhaps this is not the full story. We know that in later years John D. Rockefeller's associate Frederick Gates would level the accusation against the Hoyt Syndicate of creating false economic booms in towns where they had real estate investments.[29] In this case Gates was referring to the West Superior Iron and Steel Company, but he could also have been referring to the American Steel Barge Company, because the Land and River Improvement Company that sold the land to American Steel Barge was also owned by the Hoyt Syndicate.[30] It would seem that the major investors in the American Steel Barge Company sold the property for the new shipyard to themselves!

D. F. BARRY,   McDOUGALL WHALEBACK.   WEST SUPERIOR, WIS.

A photograph by well-known photographer David F. Barry of a whaleback steamship towing a whaleback consort barge, both loaded with a bulk cargo—the company's only successful revenue and profit generator. Source: UW-Superior Special Collections.

CHAPTER 6

The Operating Department

Unlike many other Great Lakes bulk cargo fleets of the time, which were collections of vessels each owned as a separate partnership, the American Steel Barge Company was unique because it built, owned, and managed its own ships, and investors owned shares in the company as a whole rather than in individual ships. The reason for the company to both build and operate ships is not clear. We may assume that McDougall, Hoyt, and their partners were forced to both own and operate the ships they built because established ship owners would not buy them for their fleets. However, we don't know if they were primarily interested as operators but could find no yard willing to build whaleback ships, or if they intended all along to both build and operate their ships.

Although the West Superior yard would build four ships prior to 1895 for outside interests—*Pillsbury* and *Washburn* for the Soo Line Railroad and *Pathfinder* and *Sagamore* for Pickands Mather—company records show that either customers were unhappy with the vessels as in the former case or that the company lost money building them in the latter case, so all other whaleback bulk cargo ships built prior to 1895 sailed in the American Steel Barge Company fleet.[1] One might argue that the whaleback passenger steamer *Christopher Columbus* was also built for outside interests; although it was owned by the Columbian Whaleback Steamship Company, the investors in this company were members of the Hoyt Syndicate who owned the American Steel Barge Company.

The decision to both build and operate ships had a major impact on the business. A conventional shipyard would require working capital to finance the cost of only those ships under construction and could also expect to be paid for each ship on a regular payment schedule as construction progressed. A well-managed yard could expect to turn over its working capital within the construction cycle of the ships built, but the American Steel Barge Company could only recover its capital investment as profit was earned by its ships' hauling cargo. Table 2 tabulates the cumulative cost of ships built.[2]

Year	Total Cumulative Costs	Cumulative Costs: Steamers	Cumulative Costs: Barges	Steamers as Percent Cost
\multicolumn{5}{l}{**Table 2: Cumulative Cost of Whaleback Barges and Steamships in 1892 Dollars**}
1889	$67,500	0	$67,500	0
1890	$554,700	$120,000	$434,700	22
1891	$1,562,400	$637,300	$925,100	41
1892	$2,762,956	$1,602,856	$1,160,100	58
1893	$3,540,616	$1,929,256	$1,611,360	54

The company's success, therefore, depended not on the shipyard, but on the profitability of its fleet. Its profit center was its operating department. Ships only make money when they are moving cargo, so there was an urgent need to find, load, and unload it. The term used by the American Steel Barge Company to describe this activity was "dispatch," and the company's correspondence indicates constant efforts to improve this crucial function.

Responsible for keeping the ever-growing fleet of barges and steamships moving with paying cargos was the American Steel Barge's Transportation or Operating Department. Charles Wetmore's 1892 report describes the organization that made this operation work.[3]

> *Accounting*: Charles H. Leland, age twenty-six, who, according to Wetmore's report, was "assisted by an assistant who was also a qualified Western Union and Postal cable operator."
> *Duluth*: Captain Angus McDougall (apparently not related to Alexander McDougall), general agent helped by an assistant. Wetmore wrote, "A practical lake man, responsible for the entire management of vessels on Lake Superior. Keeping track of them all the time whether on Lake Michigan … by means of daily reports and blackboard indications of the vessels. Settles questions of repair accidents, delays, and dispatch."
> *Sault Ste. Marie*: Captain A. C. Chapman. "On salary to be of all assistance

to our boats in and around the canal," Wetmore noted. Captain Chapman also owned a wrecking schooner and he was paid for it to be available to lend assistance to American Steel Barge Company vessels.

Cleveland: Captain Thomas Wilson and Captain Morton. Captain Wilson was appointed as agent to represent the company's interests at the rate of $15 per vessel handled. Wilson also owned his own fleet, the Wilson Transit Line, that towed American Steel Barge's whaleback barges. Captain Morton was retained to chase vessels in Lake Erie ports and get them dispatched. He was described by Wetmore as an "able man with only a poor education."

Buffalo: Captain George W. Bove. He handled the company's vessels on a commission basis.

Chicago: The firm of Crosby, McDonald & Company was paid a commission to handle the company's steamships. The company's barges were handled on a commission basis by the firm of Keith & Carr.

Using telegraph cables, these individuals and organizations all reported to Angus McDougall at the Duluth office. The report states: "Duluth Office being the center of dispatching point. We tried to manage this in West Superior but found it impossible, owing to the market on all freights is being made on the Duluth side."

Freight rates for bulk cargos on the Lakes fluctuated up and down depending on the laws of supply and demand and were subject to established trade customs. For example, when hauling iron ore, cargo handling was charged to the vessel at the standard rate of nineteen and one-half cents per gross ton.[4] Company records indicate that whaleback ships paid the same rate as conventional ships, despite the fact that they were supposedly more difficult to unload. On the other hand, when hauling coal, the cost to handle the cargo was borne by the consignee.[5]

At any given time there were two freight rates for bulk cargos: a contract rate and a wild rate. The wild rate reflected the rate per ton at a given moment—what today we would call the "spot market." The contract rate reflected the rate per ton for a fixed period of time. Vessel managers seeking to secure cargos could choose between tying up ships at a contract rate for a definite time period or chartering a vessel for one trip and speculating that they could take advantage of rising wild rates as the season progressed. For example, in 1891, when hauling iron ore from the Lake Superior lake head to Lake Erie ports the wild rate was $1.11 per gross ton, and the contract rate was $1.00. By 1893, the wild rate was $0.77, and the contract rate was $1.00. In other words, the wild rate in 1893 was $0.23 less than the contract rate, whereas two years earlier it had been $0.11 more than the contract rate.[6]

Table 3: Average Freight Rate, Iron Ore, Ports Named to Ohio Ports							
							Coal
	Escanaba		Marquette		Ashland and Other Ports at Head of Lake Superior		Ohio to Duluth
	Wild Rate	Contract Rate	Wild Rate	Contract Rate	Wild Rate	Contract Rate	Wild Rate
1880	$1.70	$1.83	$2.26	$2.73	-	-	-
1881	$1.35	$1.73	$2.05	$2.45			
1882	$1.04	$1.40	$1.20	$1.75			
1883	$1.22	$1.00	$1.40	$1.20			
1884	$0.67	$1.10	$1.08	$1.35			
1885	$0.78	$0.90	$0.98	$1.05	$1.25	$1.13	$0.49
1886	$1.25	$1.05	$1.31	$1.20	$1.76	$1.20	$0.78
1887	$1.59	$1.40	$1.87	$1.63	$2.25	$2.00	$0.89
1888	$1.05	$0.90	$1.30	$1.15	$1.43	$1.25	$0.66
1889	$1.01	$1.00	$1.19	$1.10	$1.34	$1.25	$0.52
1890	$0.89	$1.10	$1.07	$1.25	$1.17	$1.35	$0.49
1891	$0.84	$0.65	$1.02	$0.90	$1.11	$1.00	$0.49
1892	$0.74	$1.00	$0.98	$1.15	$1.13	$1.25	$0.43
1893	$0.56	$0.85	$0.71	$1.00	$0.77	$1.00	$0.38

Notes:

"Effective" average Duluth ore rate for 1893 was $0.941.

Although not stated in source, iron ore was customarily measured in gross tons (2,240 lbs.).

Charge to vessel for handling ore: 19.5 cents/gross ton.

Coal rate is net tons (2,000 lbs.) handled without charge to vessel.

Source: Statistics of Lake Commerce, *Marine Review*, 1894

Good operating records for the company exist for 1891.[7] From these it is possible to draw a number of interesting conclusions about the company's Great Lakes operations:

1. Eliminating vessels that were commissioned late in the season and those sent to salt water, the company operated eight barges and two steamships.

2. These ten vessels each averaged eleven trips for the season—far less than the eighteen to twenty-seven trips that Alexander McDougall considered satisfactory. It is not clear if it was difficult to convince shippers to consign cargos to the company's ships, if the company's agents were ineffective at securing them, or if the difficulty in unloading whaleback ships resulted in fewer trips.

3. It appears that the company's standard practice was to secure a cargo of coal for the return trip to the head of the lakes rather than to make the return trip in ballast. This is surprising, as many owners did not consider the return cargo offered by coal to be worthwhile—a particular disadvantage for whaleback ships that were supposedly harder to unload. As table 3 shows, freight rates for coal were considerably less than for iron ore, even taking into account the fact that the cost to unload the coal was not charged to the vessel.

4. For barges, grain produced the highest revenue per trip ($3,471). Iron ore was next ($2,090), and coal was last ($1,010). For steamships, iron ore provided more revenue per trip ($2,611) than grain ($1,938). Grain, being relatively light, is a volume cargo where the ship's internal volume would be filled before the hull reached its intended draft. Ore, on the other hand, is a weight cargo where the ship reaches its intended draft before the hold is completely filled. When hauling grain, the large volume claimed by the steamship's boilers and engine took space that a barge of similar dimensions could use to stow this light cargo. In either case, grain was an important and profitable cargo.

5. From information available, it may be inferred that the company's practice during this year was to charter its barges in the iron ore trade for most of the season at contract rates and to take advantage of the higher end-of-season wild rates for hauling two cargos of grain.

6. The company paid out $76,450 for towing vessels, indicating that by the end of 1891 it did not own enough steamships to tow its own consort barges.

There were two years, 1891 and 1892, during which the company operated normally; its building program had produced a fleet of ships, and cargo tonnages and rates were not yet affected by the 1893 economic depression. During these two years, the whaleback fleet produced significant operating profits (revenue less operating expenses and insurance). In 1891 this operating profit amounted to $153,493, and in 1892 it was $280,093. This is equivalent to $4,120,000 and $7,520,000 in 2004 dollars.[8] During each of these two years, the fleet of barges and steamships was earning approximately 10% of its initial cost, without taking into account interest expense and overhead incurred by the New York office.[9]

While it may seem that the barge line was on the road to success, earning a decent return on the value of its barges and steamships, this is not the full story. The engine that drives business is cash flow. Cash flow is the actual money available to the owners each year after all cash expenses have been paid. Cash flow differs from earnings (or net income) as non-cash bookkeeping entries that can inflate or depress earnings are eliminated. In the 1890s cash flow was possibly even more important than it is today. The only way for the owners to realize a return on their investment was through payment of cash dividends, since shares in privately held companies could not be easily traded to recoup capital gains.[10]

Table 4 illustrates the results of a highly simplified cash flow analysis for the company. Using the cost data from Alexander McDougall's account book, it was assumed that the West Superior shipyard would construct nine barges and three steamships each year. These twelve vessels would be added to the operating department's fleet in the succeeding year. Operating results for the resulting fleet of whaleback ships were developed from actual results for 1892. In other words, it was assumed that twelve ships would be built each year by the yard, and twelve, twenty-four, and thirty-six ships would be operated by the operating department in the second, third, and fourth years, and so on. In addition to insurance, overhead costs of $35,000 were assumed, based on sketchy information found in the company's financial reports. Cash flow was found to be negative in the first six years, and cumulative investment would increase to over 3.6 million (1892) dollars, not including the investment required to construct and equip the shipyard. In year seven, cash flow would turn positive and cumulative investment would begin to drop. This analysis also assumes that the company would be able to keep all vessels in the ever-growing fleet operating each year hauling cargos at profitable rates. The analysis showed that investors would have to be willing to wait until the later years of a ten-year cycle to receive any income from their investment, and that the syndicate would have to continuously raise large amounts of capital to fund construction of the new vessels built each year.

Table 4: Cash Flow Model (in US$)

Year	1	2	3	4	5	6	7	8	9	10
Operating Income	0	176,171	352,342	528,513	704,684	880,855	1,057,026	1,233,197	1,409,368	1,585,539
Overhead	35,000	35,000	35,000	35,000	35,000	35,000	35,000	35,000	35,000	35,000
Net Income	−35,000	141,171	317,342	493,513	669,684	845,855	1,022,026	1,198,197	1,374,368	1,550,539
Vessel Construction	1,012,674	1,012,674	1,012,674	1,012,674	1,012,674	1,012,674	1,012,674	1,012,674	1,012,674	1,012,674
Net Cash Flow	−1,047,674	−871,503	−695,332	−519,161	−342,990	−166,819	9,352	185,523	361,694	537,865
Cumulative Investment	1,047,674	1,919,177	2,614,509	3,133,670	3,476,660	3,643,479	3,634,127	3,448,604	3,086,910	2,549,045
Barges	0	9	18	27	36	45	54	63	72	81
Steamers	0	3	6	9	12	15	18	21	24	27
TOTAL	0	12	24	36	48	60	72	84	96	108

CHAPTER 7

Saltwater Ventures

Perhaps influenced by his earlier trip to Russia, Alexander McDougall dreamed all his life of connecting the Great Lakes to the seaborne commerce of the world. American Steel Barge Company records show that on August 14, 1889, he proposed to Colgate Hoyt that the company build a fleet of small ships to enter the Atlantic coastal coal trade.[1] The small dimensions of these ships would allow them to move back and forth through the St. Lawrence and Welland canals to take advantage of changing trade conditions.

We already know that while the Duluth yard was busy building *Barge 105* and the whaleback steamship *Colgate Hoyt*, the Hendren & Robins Atlantic Dock Company of Brooklyn, New York, launched two small whaleback barges. Built to American Steel Barge Company specifications, *Barges 201* and *202* were shorter than *Barges 102* and *103* and much shorter than the 284 ft. *Barges 104* and *105* then being built at the Duluth shipyard. Apart from their smaller size they were identical to the whaleback barges being built at McDougall's Duluth yard. With an overall length of 190 ft. these small barges were the longest vessels able to use the existing locks bypassing the rapids of the St. Lawrence River. Longer ships could "run the rapids" downstream but could not return back upstream.[2]

Other members of the Hoyt Syndicate had their own reason for wanting to use whaleback ships on salt water. They needed to move iron ore from mines that they were developing in Cuba to markets on the U.S. East Coast, so in 1891 the steamship *Joseph L. Colby* and consort *Barge 110* were sent down through the St. Lawrence River rapids to the East Coast, where they joined *Barges 201* and *202* to inaugurate the company's "Atlantic Service."[3] The importance of this new venture to the company may be gauged by the fact that the *Colby* was only the second whaleback steamship built, that there was a need for these steamers to tow the barges being produced by the new yard on the lakes, and that the company was willing to incur the additional expense of almost $3,000 to equip the ship to operate on salt water.[4]

On one saltwater voyage in 1892, the *Colby* sailed from Newport News, Virginia, apparently without a consort barge. She was loaded with 1,700 tons of cargo, probably coal as Newport News was a major East Coast coal shipping port. She unloaded her cargo at Galveston, Texas, then sailed to Cuba where she loaded 1,400 tons of iron ore from the Hoyt Syndicate mines for delivery to Philadelphia. Of particular interest is the number of days spent underway (18.5) compared to those spent in port (28.5). During that year, the ship made nine trips, so it is easy to see just how dispatch of these vessels affected profitability; of equal interest is the light load of iron ore. In his account book, McDougall claimed that the *Colby* could carry 2,129 tons deadweight on a 14 ft. draft (2,183 tons deadweight in salt water). With only 1,400 tons of cargo she would have been lightly loaded. Since she had started the voyage at Newport News with an average draft of slightly more than 14 ft., it is clear that a 14 ft. draft was allowed by the authorities that established freeboard requirements for saltwater vessels. Was this all of the ore that the mines in Cuba had to ship?[5]

As summarized in table 5, the financial results for the company's Atlantic Service were disappointing. Three factors appear to account for the poor performance: the few trips made, the small loads carried, and the high cost of insurance. As with the vessels in lake service, the company appeared to be plagued with the technicalities of operating a fleet—finding cargos, loading, unloading, clearing customs, and quarantine. The two vessels, *Barges 201* and *202*, suffered from their small size, operating at a loss in 1892.[6]

Table 5: Earnings for the American Steel Barge Company's "Atlantic Service"					
Year	Average Trips/Vessel	Gross Earnings	Insurance	Net Earnings	Return on Investment (%)
1891	11.75	$19,877	$11,578	$8,299	2.76
1892	10.25	$17,216	$18,460	−$1,244	−0.41
1893	9.25	$27,743	?	$27,743	?

Note: The return on investment is based on the cost of vessels from Alexander McDougall's "Account Book," Superior Public Museums. Other data is from American Steel Barge Company financial records for individual ships in their Atlantic Service.

The third and major factor affecting profits was the cost of insurance. For the two years that insurance costs were reported (1891 and 1892), they consumed over 80% of gross earnings. For 1893, insurance costs were not reported; perhaps the company had decided to operate without coverage.[7] Popular accounts of the whaleback ship are full of anecdotes in which McDougall outsmarted the established, conservative marine industry, but in attempting to insure his vessels, he would have been forced to deal with it head-on. Ships in saltwater commerce are transient assets. They are constantly on the move, change owners and nationality, and are subject to all sorts of hazards. The shipping industry has dealt with this by the formation of classification societies. When requested to do so by ship owners, the expert staff of these organizations review the design, construction, and maintenance of ships and assign a rating number. By looking up a ship in a classification society register, an insurance underwriter can assess risk for a vessel that might physically be on the other side of the world.

For McDougall's whalebacks to be insured for saltwater commerce, a favorable rating by one of the recognized classification societies was essential. In 1891, two such agencies were active on the U.S. East Coast: Lloyds and the American Shipmasters Association.[8] As previously discussed, the Lloyds office in Cleveland, Ohio, surveyed *Barge 102* and assigned it a favorable rating, but that was Inland Lloyds. Saltwater ships were supposed to be built to higher standards. We do not know if or how the vessels of the company's Atlantic Service were classified, but a low classification would have boosted insurance costs, and no classification would probably have made insurance impossible to obtain.

The company embarked on another saltwater venture in 1891, sending the new whaleback steamer, *C. W. Wetmore*, to England with a cargo of grain. At 264 ft. in length, the *Wetmore* could fit through the Welland Canal locks but not the smaller locks in the St. Lawrence River, so the ship ran through the river's rapids with McDougall on board. According to McDougall, the *Wetmore's* trip preceded that of the *Colby* and *Barge 110* and involved unloading the cargo into lighters at Kingston, Ontario, and reloading it below the rapids. After passing through the rapids, the ship completed her voyage across the Atlantic to England. McDougall naturally felt that this extensive saltwater voyage vindicated the oceangoing qualities of his whaleback ship design.[9]

The *Wetmore* arrived in England in June or July 1891, a time when naval architects there were debating the design of future merchant steamships. They understood that

The whaleback steamship *C. W. Wetmore*, the third such vessel built, heading down the St. Lawrence River on her maiden voyage to England. Source: Superior Public Museums.

such ships would be of riveted steel construction, would be propelled by reciprocating steam engines driving screw propellers, and would be of the largest size practicable for a given trade. Beyond that, they could not agree. The situation is well described by modern British authors Leonard Gray and John Lingwood:

> The Turret ship was a creation of that evolutionary period around the turn of the century, when sail had clearly given way to steam, yet the ideal configuration, form and size of cargo vessels had not been established.
>
> The great shipbuilding slump of the 1880s had caused many shipbuilders of the day to think seriously of the vessels that they would be required to build in the future, and in the last two decades of the 19th century a bewildering array of designs: single decked ships, well deckers, spar deckers, awning deckers, three island ships, raised quarter deckers, so called three deckers, and partial awning deckers were produced, each with variations in extent of erections and number of decks. Each design claimed to offer advantages in terms of deadweight or cubic capacity or registered tonnage, sometimes by exploiting some quirk in the current Tonnage or Load Line regulations. *Designers were groping their way towards a satisfactory balance of deadweight, capacity, stability, strength, and speed. Ship-owners and shipbuilders*

were thus ready to embrace any new design that offered any advantages over existing designs.

Considerable interest was aroused therefore by the arrival at Liverpool in 1891 after a transatlantic passage of the American "whaleback" steamer *Charles W. Wetmore*[10] (emphasis in original).

Specifically, British ship owners were interested in the *Wetmore*'s "self-trimming" characteristics as explained by English author P. N. Thomas:

> The owner of the liner trade was content with the two decked vessel as it suited his requirements best. However, the progressive tramp steamer owner was always on the lookout for ways of cutting his costs by decreasing the net register tonnage to reduce all of the dues that were based on this figure and ways to speed up loading and unloading. One of the earliest approaches adopted was "self-trimming." When a cargo steamer was loaded with a "fluid" cargo such as coal or grain, trimmers had to be employed to ensure that all spaces were filled as the cargo was loaded. If this were [*sic*] not done, the cargo would settle unevenly and would shift when the vessel rolled in rough seas. Grain settles about 5% to 6% which could leave a gap of one foot between the deck and the cargo. To counter this possibility the regulations regarding carriage of grain laid down that either the hold be filled right up to the hatch coamings which then formed a trunk to feed grain as the cargo settled or, that if the hold were not completely filled, at least two layers of grain in bags be laid over the loose grain. In the "self-trimmer" the corners of the hold at top and bottom were faired off to eliminate the possibility of empty spaces and to ensure that the top of the hold acted as one large feeder trunk.[11]

As Britain's most important outbound cargo was coal and her largest inbound cargo was grain, this was no small matter. The whaleback's curved decks eliminated the square corner between the side of the hull and the deck, improving the vessel's self-trimming characteristics. While on public display in the port city of Liverpool, the ship was scrutinized by English ship owners and their naval architects, who criticized many of the whaleback features in a technical paper presented to the Royal Institute of Naval Architects in 1892.[12] The following concerns were noted:

1. They did not like the spoon-shaped bow, as they believed that it would be damaged by slamming, which happens when a vessel pitches in a seaway. After raising to a wave crest the bow may come out of the water, so when pitching downward the bottom of the bow slams into the surface of the water. Ships with U-shaped bow hull sections are more susceptible to this than those with V-shaped bow sections and the whalebacks' spoon-shaped bow was an exaggerated U shape. What the British naval architects failed to mention was that the whalebacks were especially designed to plow through, not ride over heavy seas, thus minimizing the vessel's tendency to pitch and to slam when navigating into head seas.

2. They felt that a true self-trimming design should feature elevated cargo trunks or hatch coamings to store excess cargo that would sift down into the hold to fill voids as cargos settled. With its flush bolted hatches, *Wetmore* did not offer this feature.

3. They noted the difficult communication between bow crew quarters and stern pilothouse in rough weather.

4. They considered crew habitability inadequate for long voyages.

5. They noted the absence of auxiliary sail power. As whaleback ships were built during a period when steam machinery was subject to breakdown, ships on long voyages required an auxiliary means of propulsion.

6. They objected to the "engines aft" arrangement of American Great Lakes ships in general and whalebacks in particular, preferring the British practice of locating engines, boilers, and coal bunkers amidships.

Despite these criticisms, the English ship owning and shipbuilding community's interest in the *Wetmore* touched off a slow-motion race to build an improved sea-going whaleback steamship. The Doxford shipyard in Sunderland, England, entered the race in late 1891 when their chief draftsman, Arthur Haver, produced a design for a highly modified whaleback with a conventional bow and with McDougall's turrets replaced by a long trunk running from bow to stern. Haver apparently finalized the design for this new ship around the end of 1891. Doxford began construction of this modified whaleback vessel, identified as hull 217, sometime around April 1892. This ship, ultimately named *Turret*, was launched on November 19, 1892, and made its maiden voyage in February 1893.[13]

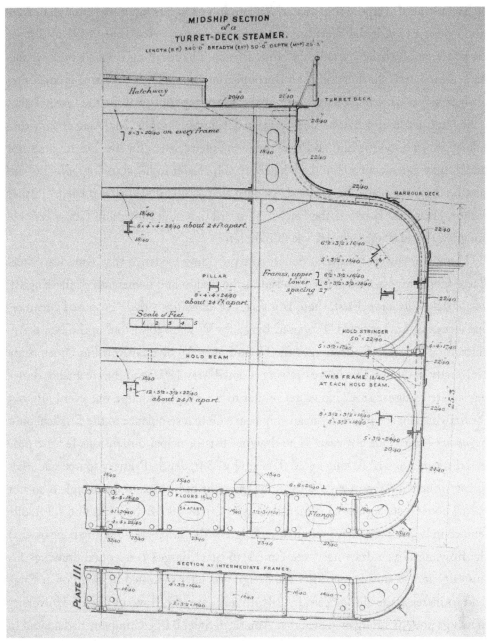

MIDSHIP SECTION
of a
TURRET-DECK STEAMER.
LENGTH (B.P.) 340'0" BREADTH (EXT) 50'0" DEPTH (MLD) 25'3"

Arrival of the *Wetmore* in England following a successful transatlantic voyage generated considerable interest among the British ship-owning community. One English shipbuilder responded with an improved whaleback, known as the turret ship. This midship drawing shows the essential feature of this highly successful vessel. The row of hatches bolted flush to the whaleback's deck has been replaced with a trunk, called a turret, running the length of the deck. The hatches are elevated above the sea, allowing for wooden hatch covers that are more easily handled. The turret also adds considerable longitudinal strength to the hull, correcting a major problem affecting the whalebacks—their weak deck structure. Source: Holms, Practical Shipbuilding, 1916.

Meanwhile, Liverpool ship owner William Johnston was interested enough in *Wetmore*'s design to visit the West Superior shipyard in early November 1891 to discuss construction of whaleback ships in Great Britain. The resulting English-built whaleback, *Sagamore*, is shrouded in confusion and controversy. Even the name is confusing as there was a whaleback barge built at the West Superior yard for the Great Lakes bulk cargo trade also named *Sagamore*. In his autobiography, McDougall says that Johnston came to visit him and that they remained friends for life, but he does not mention an agreement to build a whaleback ship. Later in his autobiography he says that he drew the plans for a whaleback ship that William Johnston owned.[14] Other authors claim that Doxford, the English shipyard that built *Turret* and *Sagamore*, stole American Steel Barge's whaleback ship design.[15]

There are, however, archival documents providing evidence that American Steel Barge Company was integrally involved in the design and ownership of the English whaleback, *Sagamore*. First, there is a series of drawings titled "Proposed Steamer" and a companion set titled "Proposed Barge for William Johnston" in the Naval Architectural Drawing Collection of the Great Lakes Archives at Bowling Green State University in Ohio.[16] The barge drawing is dated May 1892, and the steamship drawing is dated August 1892. No vessel similar to the proposed barge was ever built, but the drawings for the proposed steamship bear a close resemblance to the English-built *Sagamore*—close but not exact. The drawing lists principal dimensions for the proposed steamer as 312 ft. long by 36 ft. beam by 25 ft. depth. Primary source materials listing principal dimensions for the ship have not been located, but English author P. N. Thomas lists *Sagamore*'s dimensions as 311 ft. by 38.2 ft. by 25 ft. The 2.2 ft. difference in beam would have required redesign of the ship.[17] It therefore appears that the Bowling Green drawings were American Steel Barge's conceptual drawings for this saltwater steamship, and that the design was later modified by them or in England to increase the ship's beam by 2 ft. In any case, the Bowling Green University drawings present strong evidence that American Steel Barge Company had a hand in designing this saltwater whaleback steamer. For a drawing of this proposed steamship, see plate 3.

American Steel Barge Company's financial records provide additional evidence that the company was involved in the *Sagamore* project. Company cash flow projections for the second half of 1892 include cash requirements of $75,000 for the "Johnston contract." In a later projection for the same year, future cash requirements for the

Johnston contract were reduced to $50,000, implying that a payment of $25,000 had been made. As McDougall could build a whaleback steamship in 1892 for $175,000, $75,000 would have purchased a significant interest in this English-built vessel. It is hard to imagine why else American Steel Barge would have owed this large sum to William Johnston.[18] Strangely, however, ledger accounts that record the company's assets and liabilities for the period make no mention of the Johnston contract. In mid-1892 American Steel Barge, in addition to participating in construction of the *Sagamore*, attempted to promote its whaleback ships by forming an English company, the Whaleback Steamship Company Ltd.[19] Financial records for late 1892 list this company as an $18,333 asset, and a cash flow forecast for the same period estimated that this subsidiary company would require an additional cash investment of $165,000 during 1893, so perhaps funds paid or anticipated to be paid to William Johnston are included in these numbers.[20]

The final piece of evidence is a news article in the *Duluth Evening Herald* dated February 14, 1893. This article announced that the American Steel Barge Company would have two vessels, a whaleback steamship and consort barge, built in England "at or near Liverpool." Dimensions for the steamer would be the same as the *James Colgate* except two feet deeper. *Colgate*'s register dimensions were 308 ft. by 38 ft. by 24 ft. The two vessels were intended for the Cuba–Philadelphia iron ore trade and were to be fitted with pole masts similar to the *Joseph Colby*. The vessels would sail under the British flag and would be ready to receive their first cargo in mid-1893.[21]

One highly regarded English author claims that the *Sagamore* was owned by the Belgian-American Maritime Company, a 50/50 partnership between William Johnston and Doxford. This would preclude American Steel Barge Company ownership, but it is implausible that Doxford would willingly invest in the American-designed ship if it was already building an improved whaleback ship—a turret ship—of its own design.[22]

In any event, the *Sagamore* was built not at or near Liverpool but at Sunderland, the shipbuilding center in northeast England, by the same Doxford shipyard that was building the turret ships. It seems unlikely that William Johnston would have awarded his contract to a shipyard building a vessel that would compete with his, but that is what he did. The Doxford organization was, however, well known to Alexander McDougall and the American Steel Barge Company. Earlier, on April 20, 1891, the *Superior Daily Call* reported that American Steel Barge had purchased the engine for the whaleback steamship *E. B. Bartlett* from Doxford, so perhaps McDougall, familiar with this English shipbuilder, directed Johnston to place the order for construction of the English-built whaleback steamship with them.[23] Nevertheless, Doxford accepted Johnston's order and assigned it hull number 218.[24]

Although the evidence is confusing, I believe a plausible explanation of the circumstances surrounding the construction of this English-built whaleback is that William Johnston was impressed by the arrival of the *C. W. Wetmore* in Britain. He then traveled to West Superior, Wisconsin, in November 1891 to meet with the American Steel Barge Company.[25] During this meeting the two companies discussed construction of whaleback ships in England. After returning to England, Johnston learned that the Doxford shipyard was already constructing an improved whaleback, the turret ship. During the summer of 1892, American Steel Barge established an English subsidiary company, funded the company in the amount of $18,333, and provided preliminary designs to William Johnston for a whaleback steamship and consort barge.

In November/December 1892 William Johnston again journeyed to West Superior, Wisconsin.[26] This visit resulted in a firm deal to build in England a whaleback steamship and consort barge that would be used to haul iron ore from the Hoyt Syndicate's Cuban iron ore mines to markets near Philadelphia. This deal was announced in February 1893. These vessels, flying the British flag, could have been owned by American Steel Barge's new English subsidiary and managed by William Johnston. Johnston then placed an order with the Doxford organization to build the two vessels. His reasons for choosing the Doxford yard are unknown, but Alexander McDougall might have urged him to do so.

The American Steel Barge Company's operations were curtailed in 1893 when John D. Rockefeller assumed control of the company (see chapter 9). Since the Cuban iron ore mines were involved in Rockefeller's consolidation of the American iron mining industry, operations there may have been suspended, eliminating the need for the English-built whaleback vessels. William Johnston and the Doxford shipyard may well have been stuck with the whaleback steamship under construction. Compounding their problem was the fact that Lloyds, the English classification society, refused to accept the whaleback design. Johnston and Doxford apparently decided to finish the steamship *Sagamore*, to classify her with the European Bureau Veritas, to operate her under the Belgian flag, and to organize a Belgian company to own her.[27] Whatever termination agreement they negotiated with American Steel Barge was amicable enough to allow McDougall to remain personally friendly with William Johnston.[28] The consort barge appears to have never been laid down, as succeeding Doxford hull numbers are for turret ships.

While the *Wetmore* had been designed for Great Lakes service, the *Sagamore* represented an attempt to build a true ocean-going whaleback steamship. In his study of tramp steamships, English author P. N. Thomas published an inboard profile drawing for the *Sagamore* that closely resembles that shown in the Bowling Green archives.[29] This design attempted to satisfy most of the criticisms of the Royal Institute of Naval Architects. Masts for handling cargo and for setting sails were included, and an elevated catwalk improved fore and aft access. Cylindrical turrets were located between hatches acting as standpipes to improve self-trimming characteristics. Habitability was improved by moving crew's quarters from the forecastle aft to a cabin elevated on turrets. The ship's cargo holds were also fitted with a tween deck, an intermediate deck between the doublebottom and main deck, to facilitate carriage of package freight that would be damaged if stacked too high.

The most significant change in the design of the ship involved arrangement of the cargo holds. Great Lakes whalebacks located all cargo holds forward of the ship's propulsion machinery. The *Sagamore*'s designers located one cargo hold in the stern and moved her machinery forward with the propeller shaft passing through a shaft alley running through this aft hold. The reason for placing this cargo hold in a less advantageous location and for incurring the additional cost, and loss of cargo space, for a shaft alley was to better control the ship's longitudinal trim.[30]

Steamships sailing the Great Lakes were never far from a supply of coal for fuel. Coaling facilities were located in the discharge ports along the lower lakes, at Duluth, and at Sault Ste. Marie. Because ships were never more than 300–400 miles from a fuel source, coal bunkers could be small.[31] Ocean-going ships, however, required coal bunkers that could hold coal for voyages of thousands of miles. With engines located aft and coal bunkers necessarily nearby, changes in longitudinal trim would occur as the bunkers were emptied. If these trim changes were large, the propeller could become uncovered as the ship pitched, causing the engine to over-speed. We know from company records that the *Colby* lost her propeller on a saltwater voyage, possibly from engine over-speeding.[32]

The *Sagamore*'s machinery arrangement allowed her designers to move the large variable weight of her coal bunkers closer to her longitudinal center of buoyancy where emptying them would lessen changes in trim. Not all English naval architects agreed with this argument. The author of the 1892 Royal Institute of Naval Architect's paper claimed that the English practice of locating propulsion machinery amidships was no longer necessary, as improvements in steam engine efficiency had drastically reduced fuel consumption.[33]

The *Sagamore* was launched by Doxford on June 15, 1893, seven months after it launched its own *Turret*, and although the *Sagamore* proved to be a seaworthy cargo hauler, American Steel Barge had lost the race to build an improved saltwater whale-back steamship.[34]

While continuing to reject the whaleback design, Lloyds did eventually agree to clas-sify the Doxford turret ship.[35] The turret ship design was not without its faults—with the turret full of cargo, the ships had a nasty tendency to capsize, but they were cheap to operate.[36] Many costs associated with operation of tramp steamships, particularly Suez Canal tolls, were based on register tonnage, and English tramp steamer operators believed that to be efficient a vessel's deadweight, a rough indicator of its cargo hauling capacity, should be at least 2.4 times her net register tonnage. By taking advantage of a loophole in British tonnage regulations, register tonnages for turret ships were small in proportion to cargo carried. The deadweight of the *Turret*, Doxford's first turret ship, was 2.53 times her net register tonnage, and succeeding ships were better still. By contrast, the *Sagamore*'s deadweight was only 1.86 times her net register tonnage, so she did not compare favorably.[37] By aggressively marketing their turret ship design, employing modern concepts like accepting old ships in trade and financing new ships, and instructing owners how to properly load their vessels, Doxford sold the turret ship design to English ship owners and over 170 were eventually built.[38]

The *Sagamore* successfully hauled cargo for William Johnston until she was sold to Italian owners in 1911. She often traded back and forth to the Black Sea and Eastern Mediterranean. Sunk by a German submarine in 1917, she was the only whaleback ship not built in the United States.[39]

Another saltwater venture was the Pacific Steel Barge Company, established to own and operate whaleback ships on the Pacific Ocean and to build them at a new ship-yard at Everett, Washington, on land owned by the Hoyt Syndicate.[40] While capable of building large ships that could be launched directly into salt water, the yard was located in a frontier settlement where all shipbuilding materials had to be delivered by sea from San Francisco. Long-haul rail access from the Midwest would not be available until 1893, when James J. Hill's Great Northern Railway was completed. This is certainly an example of Gates's indictment of alleged booming of towns in which the Hoyt Syndicate owned property.[41]

The isolation of this new shipbuilding settlement was emphasized by the next voyage of the *Charles W. Wetmore*. Upon her return to the U.S. East Coast, the ship was loaded with machinery for the shipyard and for other industries planned for the new settlement, though loading large industrial equipment aboard a freighter with small hatches designed to haul bulk cargos must have been difficult. The *Wetmore* then proceeded to sail around Cape Horn to the U.S. West Coast. En route, she suffered a serious breakdown. Somewhere off the U.S. West Coast her rudder failed, probably due to corrosion caused by the saltwater environment as previously mentioned. After drifting, perhaps attempting to use her auxiliary sail rig that had been patented by McDougall to satisfy criticisms of British naval architects, the *Wetmore* was taken in tow by the steamer *Zambesi* and brought into Astoria, Oregon. This incident generated a large salvage claim, listed on Pacific Steel Barge's books as a $35,991.08 cost.[42]

After unloading her cargo of equipment and building materials, the *Wetmore* was transferred to the books of the Pacific Steel Barge Company, where she was carried at a value of $200,000. Since she originally cost $131,800, and since the American Steel Barge Company owned the stock of Pacific Steel Barge, this transaction would have netted the parent company a paper profit of $68,200, but it did nothing to improve either company's cash position.[43] Placed in the coal trade, her life as a West Coast bulk carrier was short. On September 8, 1893, she stranded off Coos Bay, Oregon. Salvage attempts failed, and she was declared a total loss a little more than eight months after her December 21, 1891, arrival at Everett.[44]

Using the equipment and materials delivered by the *Wetmore*, the Pacific Steel Barge Company built one whaleback steamship, the *City of Everett*, launched on October 24, 1894.[45] In designing this interesting vessel, the company's engineering department appears to have tried to build a real saltwater vessel, correcting some of the problems identified by the English naval architects and by operating the *Wetmore* on the high seas. As with the *Sagamore*, the *City of Everett* featured a raised turret at each hatch and an elevated catwalk stretching from the foremost turret to the deckhouse aft. There were four masts for setting auxiliary sails and for handling cargo. Machinery was located aft. There was no hold aft of the machinery as on the *Sagamore*, but the coal bunker was moved forward of the crew quarters, and the pilothouse was located

WHALEBACK CHARLES W. WETMORE AT DOCK AT LOWELL IN 1891
EVERETT HISTORICAL SERIES N° 18   Courtesy   BERGMAN & FOLLESTAD

Unloading of the *C. W. Wetmore* after her epic but difficult voyage around Cape Horn to the new West Coast settlement of Everett, Washington. The *Wetmore* is delivering a cargo of machinery for shipbuilding and other industries planned for the town. Source: UW-Superior Special Collections.

atop its own turret forward of the bunkers. This would have allowed for more fuel capacity while reducing changes in trim. This arrangement was repeated in 1896 on the Great Lakes whaleback steamship *Frank Rockefeller*, so it must have been satisfactory. The *City of Everett*'s principal dimensions were 365 ft. in length overall, a 42 ft. beam, and 22.9 ft. in depth. Her forced draft boilers feeding steam to her triple expansion steam engine were state-of-the-art in 1894 and would have reduced fuel consumption on long voyages.[46]

Unlike the *Wetmore*, the *City of Everett* had a long productive career. She traded throughout the Pacific, passed through the Suez Canal, and on one voyage circumnavigated the world. In the late 1890s she was added to John D. Rockefeller's ocean-going fleet carrying petroleum products. In 1903 she suffered a catastrophic fire while docked in Port Arthur, Texas. She was rebuilt and continued sailing until she was lost with all hands in 1923 while crossing the Gulf of Mexico.[47]

The *City of Everett* was the only vessel built at the Everett, Washington, shipyard. In the consolidation of the American Steel Barge Company that occurred during the

Panic of 1893, the yard was closed.[48] In discussing the settlement at Everett, Washington, Alexander McDougall writes:

> When the site at Everett was chosen, preparations were made at once to establish a city, start manufacturers, and create a port of the first magnitude. A shipyard was to be among the first enterprises, and to stimulate interest it was decided to send a whaleback there with the first cargo of building materials.[49]

In other words, one reason for sending the *Wetmore* on her saltwater voyages was to publicize the whaleback ships that the American Steel Barge Company was attempting to sell. Unfortunately, this publicity scheme backfired. The *Wetmore* was only the third whaleback steamship built, and although her propulsion machinery would have been equipped to operate in salt water, she was not designed as a saltwater steamship. Her poor performance and short life is in contrast to the long, productive lives enjoyed by the *Sagamore* and the *City of Everett*, the two whaleback steamships especially designed for salt water.

In addition, the *Wetmore* was not the best whaleback steamship that the company could have sent. The *Wetmore* was the first of three canal-sized, sister whaleback steamships launched by the company in the summer of 1891. But these ships were not quite sisters. The *Wetmore* was equipped with a compound engine. Her two sister whaleback steamships were built with much more efficient triple expansion engines. Specifically, the *A. D. Thompson*, equipped with an American-built triple expansion engine, was launched two weeks after the *Wetmore*, and the *E. B. Bartlett* with a Doxford triple expansion engine, was launched six weeks after the *Wetmore*.[50] While ships with compound engines could easily travel the short distances on the Great Lakes, the fuel savings gained with a triple expansion engine allowed the ships on long voyages to travel farther between fueling. Triple expansion engines had been considered the industry standard for ships in deep-sea service since the mid-1880s, so sending a compound powered steamship to England in 1891 only served to reinforce the idea to the ship owning community that their American cousins were technically unsophisticated.[51]

The *Wetmore*'s high-profile arrival in England may have grabbed the attention of the English shipping community, but they soon became only too aware of her West Coast rudder failure, as this was discussed in the Royal Institute of Naval Architect's whaleback paper. A modern English maritime historian sums up their opinion by saying "Their fears were justified as the steamer was badly knocked about on her return voyage, as she rounded Cape Horn and was wrecked shortly after on the Oregon Coast."[52]

The argument can therefore be made that the American Steel Barge Company's campaign to sell whaleback steamships in Great Britain foundered when the American Steel Barge Company failed to put its best foot forward by selecting the *Charles W. Wetmore* for long saltwater voyages.

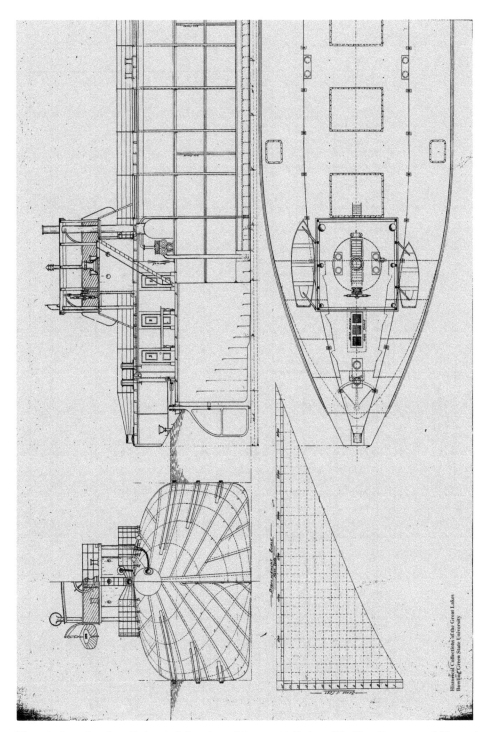

Plate 1a, b, and c. A well-detailed drawing of *Barge 102*, Robert Clark's refinement of Alexander McDougall's primitive *Barge 101*. The body plan at the upper left corner of the drawing shows the changes made in hull form to improve performance. The more circular sections at the bow would increase buoyancy, and the graceful wineglass-shaped sections aft would improve flow to the rudder. All succeeding whaleback barges built on the Great Lakes prior to 1896 would be built to this highly successful design—either duplicates or "stretched" versions that were enlarged by adding frames to the parallel midbody of the hull. Source: Bowling Green State University Special Collections.

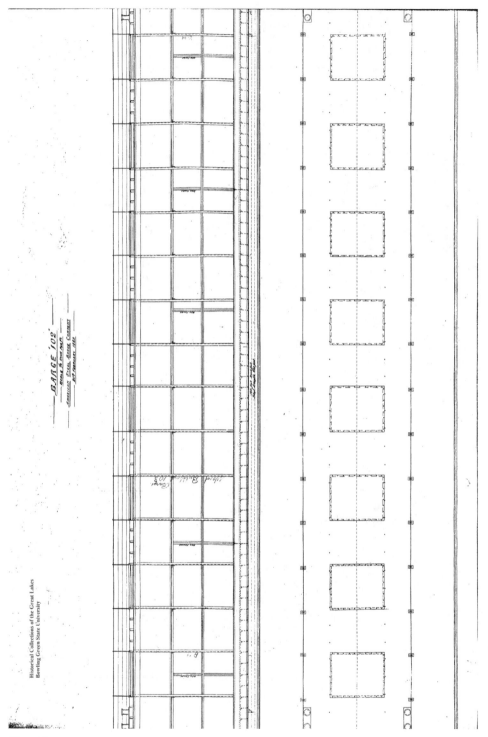

BARGE '102'

Plate 1b

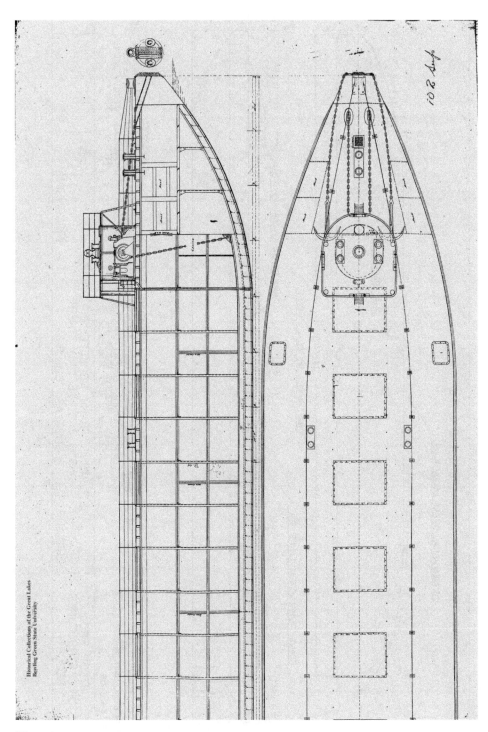

Plate 1c

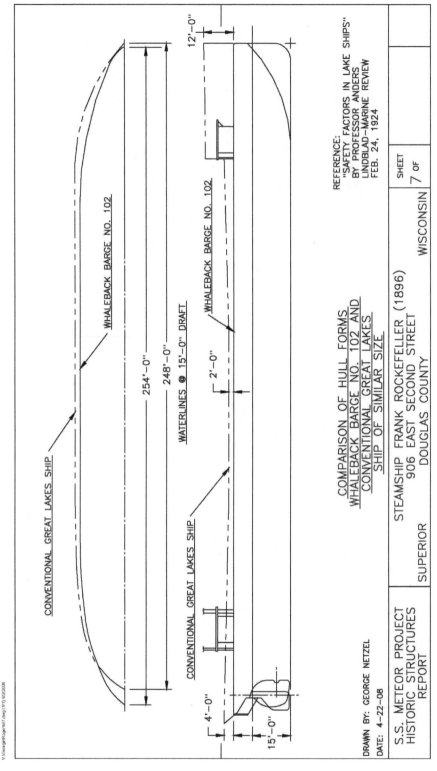

Plate 2. A drawing that compares a steamship of whaleback design to a conventionally designed vessel of similar dimensions. Source: Superior Public Museums.

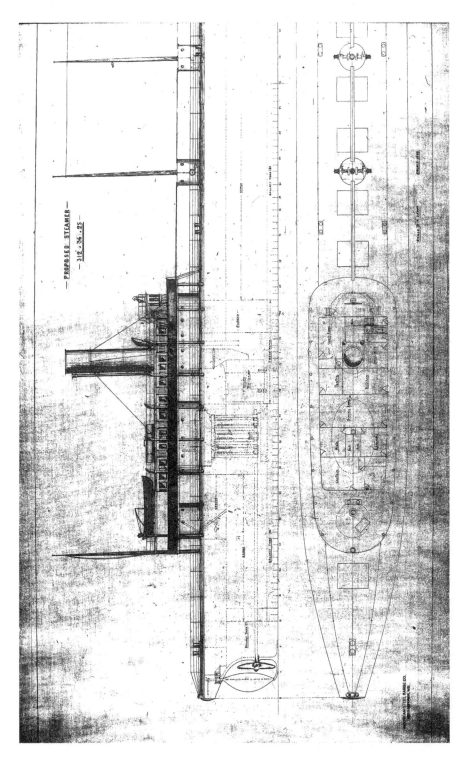

Plate 3a and b. American Steel Barge Company's attempt to adapt their whaleback design for saltwater service. Steel standpipes have been added between the rectangular hatches to provide feeding capacity for fluid cargos such as grain. Masts have been added to permit sails to be set in the event of a mechanical breakdown, and an elevated gangway connects the forward turret with the aft deck structure improving communication between the crew's quarters in the bow and the machinery, navigation station, and ship's galley in the stern. This drawing probably represents the preliminary design for the English-built whaleback steamship *Sagamore*. Source: Bowling Green State University Special Collections.

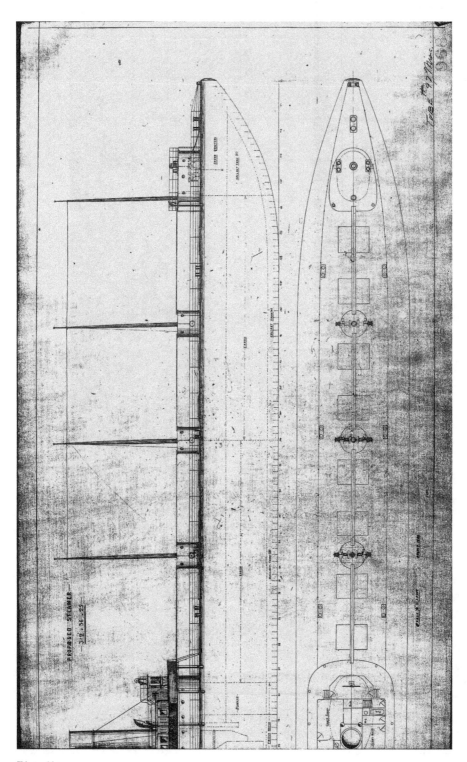

Plate 3b

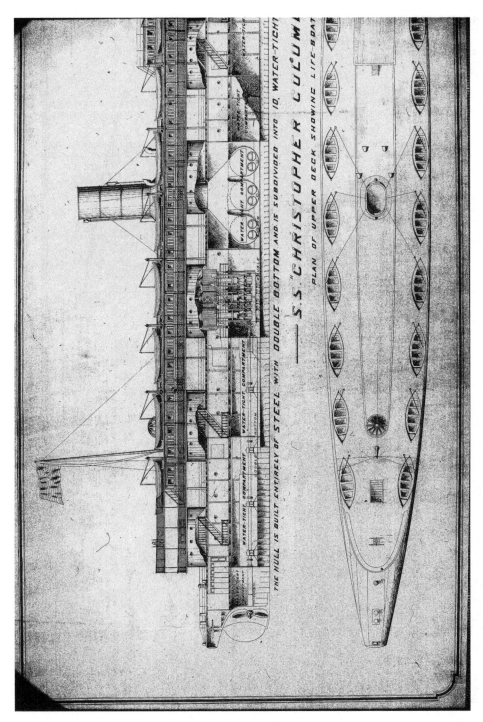

Plate 4a and b. An internal profile of the passenger steamship *Christopher Columbus*. Probably intended as a promotional rather than a technical drawing, it touts her many watertight compartments, full double bottom, and lifeboats—although with a passenger capacity in the thousands, there are clearly not enough lifeboats for all. The stairways from the gangways in the hull up through the turrets to the elevated passenger accommodations are clearly shown. Source: Bowling Green State University Special Collections.

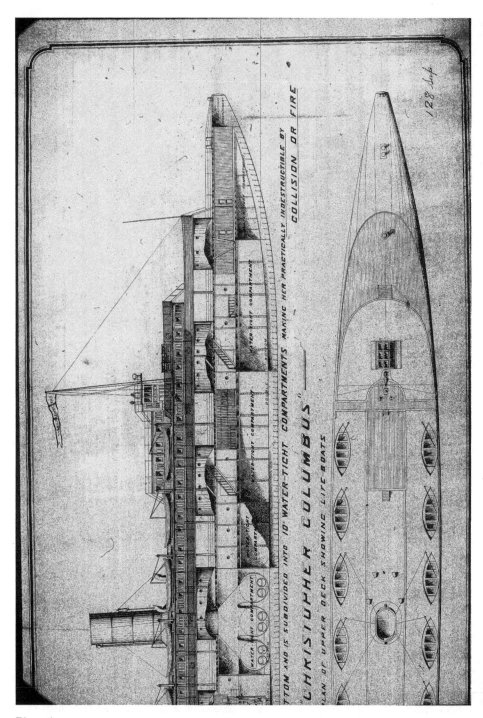

Plate 4b

The West Superior shipyard in its heyday with whaleback barges and steamships under construction. Although the large ship assembly shed was a notable feature of the yard, these vessels are being built out in the open. Source: Bowling Green State University Special Collections-Entry 933.

CHAPTER 8

Heyday

Of the forty whaleback ships built by the American Steel Barge Company on the Great Lakes, nineteen were launched during the heyday years of 1891–1892. All but five of these were built for the company's own fleet.[1] Robert Clark's refinement of Alexander McDougall's whaleback concept for barges and steamships was so successful that, except for designing a few special-purpose vessels, yard management's major problems were those associated with producing ships to Clark's standardized designs: obtaining materials, managing labor, and maintaining schedules.

The company's ability to control costs and maintain schedules was complicated by its remote location and by the fact that it did not build engines or boilers.[2] This equipment had to be procured from manufacturers on the lower lakes and shipped to

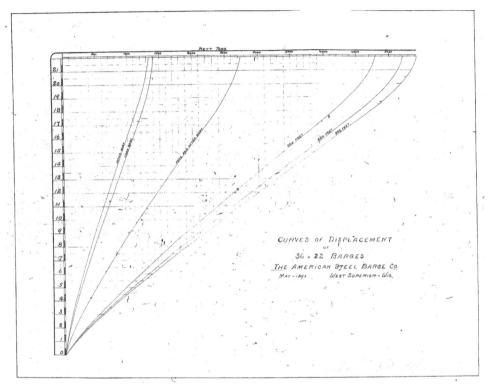

A displacement scale for whaleback barges. This scale plots displacement (horizontal scale) against the vessel's mean draft (vertical scale). While such scales were commonly used by shippers and steamship operators to determine cargo capacity, this scale includes an added feature. Separate curves are included for the vessels' fore body and after body. This would permit displacement for any length barge with 36 ft. by 22 ft. midsection dimension to be quickly determined by adding fore and after body displacement to the displacement for the midsection. For this to work, fore and after body hull lines for all barges with 36 ft. by 22 ft. midship dimensions had to be identical. Source: Bowling Green State University Special Collections.

the West Superior yard over the lakes, which of course froze each winter. The yard was served by rail, but it is unknown if the railroads could handle these large, heavy items.

Even the shipbuilding steel had to be purchased through brokers in Cleveland, though later these materials were furnished locally by the West Superior Iron and Steel Company, another Hoyt Syndicate enterprise.[3] In his autobiography, McDougall tells of the first hull plates for the passenger steamer *Christopher Columbus* arriving at the shipyard "warm from the rolling mill, accompanied by a brass band and all Superior behind it."[4]

To build these ships in a short time frame, the American Steel Barge Company used standardized designs that maximized duplicate parts. Excluding several unique vessels discussed below, all barges and steamships built during this period were produced in only two beam/depth combinations. All of the barges plus the steamship *Joseph Colby* were built with a beam/depth combination of 36 ft. by 22 ft. The six additional steamships utilized a beam/depth combination of 38 ft. by 24 ft.[5] For a tabulation of whaleback vessels arranged by beam/depth dimensions, see appendix B.

Hull frame patterns were duplicated for all vessels with a given beam/depth combination, as were bow and stern lines. Steamships were the exception, where a different stern design was necessary to accommodate the propeller.[6] Ships of different lengths with a given beam/depth combination were produced by simply adding or deleting frames within the parallel midbody section of the hull. As all whaleback barges and steamships had long parallel midbodies and no sheer, most of the hull frames were also exact duplicates. This duplication of components made for efficient production work.

During this period of rapid production, the company built seven barges and four steamships, which at 264 ft. long could pass through the existing Welland Canal around Niagara Falls and would fit into the chambers of the proposed 270 ft. long St. Lawrence River locks. Not everyone at the American Steel Barge Company agreed with construction of these small vessels. Robert Clark wrote of the three "canal-sized" steamships built in 1891: "During 1892 [*sic*] three similar whaleback steamers were built at the West Superior yard of the American Steel Barge Company. Those three vessels were built to go through the Welland Canal locks, which were then the only way out to the sea. Had they been built for the Lakes, they might have been over 300 ft. long and more profitable."[7]

As long as he was active in the company, McDougall would continue to campaign for small ships, claiming them to be easier to handle in the small harbors of the Great Lakes. Events would ultimately prove him to be wrong.[8]

The decks for all whaleback ships built after *Barge 101* were elliptical in cross section. The height of this elliptical shape was restricted by the geometry of the existing iron ore loading docks. As wider ships were built, this elliptical shape had to become flatter (the major axis of the ellipse became longer in relation to the minor axis) to maintain the slope of the loading spouts from the docks.

Following Clark's design of *Barge 102*, all succeeding whaleback ships were built with a doublebottom or water bottom. By the 1890s British ships were being built with cellular doublebottoms of interlocking fore and aft members, but McDougall

A photograph of a whaleback vessel under construction, clearly showing its internal structure. The closely spaced horizontal members that frame the ship's bottom are called floors by naval architects. Running longitudinally on top of the floors are the girders that form the McIntyre tank structure. The angled structure running fore and aft is called the margin plate. This connects the inner bottom structure to the side framing. All of this structure would be plated over to form a watertight tank over the vessel's bottom. The vertical side framing is clearly visible, along with the widely spaced heavier vertical web frames. The longitudinal stringers that are riveted to the web frames and back up the lighter side framing are also visible. Source: Superior Public Museums.

used the McIntyre system, an earlier structural design common on the Great Lakes but obsolete in Britain.[9] In this design, a system of continuous longitudinal girders was riveted to the top of the transverse floors. The tanktop plating was riveted to the top of these girders. The McIntyre design would have provided a deeper (by the height of the longitudinal girders) doublebottom than the more modern cellular design.

Doublebottoms were an important feature on ships trading on the Great Lakes, as these vessels often ran aground in the shallow channels, damaging their bottom plating. Great Lakes ships, whalebacks included, were usually designed to float with their doublebottoms flooded. Doublebottoms would increase capacity to store water ballast and would increase the height of the ship's center of gravity when loaded with cargo, providing an easier motion in a seaway.

In one of his many patents, No. 456,586, dated July 28, 1891, McDougall claimed that the structural framing utilized for his whaleback barges and steamships provided a "framework which will be very strong and rigid and at the same time, simple and capable of being set up easily."[10] Others have also claimed that the structural system used for the whalebacks allowed for a lighter hull for given displacement. The two major features claimed in McDougall's patents included a heavy keel/keelson assembly and a double-riveted angle iron assembly (also known as a "Z" bar) that ran continuously around the hull transversely to form an integrated deck beam and side frame. These two angles split at the top of the innerbottom, one running along the margin plate and the other continuing clear to the keel and riveted to the floor. These two angles formed a continuous ring that could be assembled flat on the ground and set up in one piece. This assembly eliminated the reinforced "knee" joint between the deck and side framing found in conventional ships, resulting in a light deck structure.

While McDougall's structural scheme might have simplified construction of these ships, it demonstrated a lack of understanding of structural design principles on the part of both McDougall and Clark. This is not surprising, as neither man is known to have received any training in structural engineering.[11]

Since the 1860s naval architects have realized that ship hulls were really giant box girders subject to the downward forces caused by the weight of hull, machinery, and cargo and the upward force of buoyancy. Distribution of downward forces is dependent on the location of weights in the ship's hull. For example, the ship's boilers represent a large concentrated weight at a specific location, and a bulk cargo represents a weight distributed over an area.

Upward buoyancy force is dependent on underwater hull shape. Although total weight must equal total buoyancy, the fact that these forces do not act equally at every point along the ship's longitudinal axis causes a bending action along the hull called a "bending moment." This effect is exacerbated when the ship travels through waves that increase or decrease buoyancy at points along the hull. Wave crests at bow and stern increase buoyancy at these points relative to midship, causing a condition known as "sagging." A wave crest at midship results in a lack of buoyancy at bow and stern and an excess of buoyancy midship, a condition known as "hogging."

The deck of a ship hull in the sagging condition is in compression, while the ship's bottom is in tension. In the hogging condition, the effect is the opposite; the deck is in tension while the bottom is in compression. A ship hull traveling through waves is, therefore, alternately hogging and sagging with deck and bottom alternately in tension and compression. Since stresses and strains in deck and bottom are always opposite, there must be a point along the side of the ship's hull that is neither in compression or tension. This is called the neutral axis.[12]

The longitudinal structure of the ship's hull resists these tensile and compressive stresses, and its arrangement determines the hull's ability to withstand hogging and sagging. However, with their intentionally light deck structures and heavy McIntyre doublebottoms, the neutral axes of the whaleback ships were located closer to the bottom of the hull, resulting in higher stresses on the decks, which were also not as strong as the doublebottom. In other words, the ships' bottoms were too strong relative to the decks.

Adding to the problem was the curved shape of the whaleback deck, which was less able to withstand longitudinal bending loads than a flat deck of the same thickness with a reinforced angle section between deck and side.[13]

Another ill-chosen design for the whaleback barges and steamships was the massive keel mentioned in the patent. In designing their ships in this way, Clark and McDougall were unnecessarily imitating a construction detail of wooden sailing ships that relied on the keel structure (sometimes as high as 7 ft.) to resist bending forces.[14] Because a steel ship's hull plates and other structural members were tightly joined together by riveting, designers could utilize the strength of hull, deck, and bottom plating to withstand bending moments without resorting to such massive keels. A light keel structure designed only to withstand loads imposed by dry-docking the ship would have been sufficient. The heavy keel moved the ship's neutral axis even farther down by adding strength to the bottom structure that was already strengthened by the McIntyre doublebottom, again increasing stresses in the deck. Evidence of the whalebacks' poor structural design was provided later, when a number of ships sold for service on salt water experienced buckling of decks and fracturing of deck rivets.[15]

Stresses caused by longitudinal bending of a ship's hull are called primary stresses. Ships are of course subject to all sorts of other loadings that can cause stresses in the vessel's hull structure. While these are called secondary stresses by naval architects, they can be quite serious, causing severe damage or loss of the ship. For example, secondary stresses caused the loss of the *Titanic* when hull plates or riveted hull seams failed after she sideswiped an iceberg.

Ships traversing the Great Lakes are particularly susceptible to navigational hazards that can damage hull plates, riveted seams, and other hull structural members.

Many harbors are small, channels are narrow and shallow, and the several locks require careful navigation. Even today, with modern electronic navigation equipment, hull damage is not unheard of. Furthermore, all ship hulls are affected by the hydrostatic pressure of the water that floats them.

To reinforce the sides of the hulls to withstand these loads, the side framing of the whaleback ships was built using the web frame system. This system, common on the lakes, utilized heavy web frames spaced every 12 ft. with lighter transverse frames at regular intervals in between. Running longitudinally between webs and supporting the lighter hull frames were intercostal (noncontinuous) stringers. These stringers were intended to assist the transverse frames to withstand hydrostatic pressure and local loads from collisions with docks, lock walls, and other obstacles. The stringers were riveted to each of the transverse frames to prevent the frame from twisting under load. This system originated in Britain and is described in British shipbuilding books.[16]

To withstand hydrostatic pressure loadings, shipbuilders of the time wished to limit the unsupported vertical span of hull frames to about 7 ft. This would have required many beams passing horizontally through the hold of the ship; the web frame system allowed elimination of some but not all of these hold beams.[17] One row of horizontal beams was provided on whaleback barges and steamships to withstand the force of water pressing against the sides of the hull. These hold beams were located at the point where the straight hull side intersected with the curved deck. Two rows of vertical stanchions were erected within the whaleback cargo hold to support the decks and to keep hull sections from distorting as the ship flexed in a seaway. All of this internal structure interfered with unloading of bulk cargo but was considered necessary by naval architects, and it was typically installed in all Great Lakes ships built during the period, whaleback and otherwise.[18]

A surprising amount of wood was used to construct whaleback barges and steamships. In accordance with McDougall's concept to build inexpensive vessels, wood was used for the cabins and pilothouse built on top of the aft turrets. Unlike a conventional vessel, where skilled ship joiners had to contend with a surface curved in two directions (longitudinal sheer and transverse deck camber), the area atop the turret was flat, simplifying construction by less-skilled carpenters.

Bulkheads dividing the cargo holds were also constructed of wood and were not watertight; they served only to separate cargo when necessary. This standard Great Lakes practice was criticized by naval architects elsewhere who argued that cargo

An example of Alexander McDougall's patented anchors used aboard his whaleback barges and steamships. This particular example is from the sunken whaleback steamship *Thomas Wilson*. It is on display at the Lake Superior Maritime Visitor Center in Duluth's Canal Park. While this anchor, with its central fluke that flopped back and forth to dig into the bottom, foreshadowed similar lightweight Danforth anchors that would be developed years later, it had one limitation—it was not self-stowing. Unlike the stockless anchors being developed at the same time that could be hoisted directly into pockets in the hull, McDougall's had to be catted. As the anchor broke the surface of the water a separate tackle had to be hooked to it to pull it into position for stowage—a dangerous procedure. Source: Superior Public Museums.

holds should be subdivided to prevent flooding of a single compartment from sinking the ship.[19]

All whaleback barges were fitted with a rectangular rudder that was hinged to the vessel's sternpost. The steamships were fitted with the patented elliptical-shaped balanced rudder discussed earlier.

Each steamship required a well-designed steam plant for propulsion, and each barge required steam-powered machinery to pump bilges and ballast water, operate the windlass to handle the anchor and tow lines, and in some cases to operate steam steering gear. Installation of boilers, piping, and equipment must therefore have been an important engineering job, as the eighteen steamships built by the American Steel Barge Company utilized at least eleven machinery designs. Although the company did not actually build steam engines, boilers, or pumps, their marine engineering department was responsible for integrating these components into an efficient, reliable

A Scotch marine boiler being shipped from the Duluth Boiler Works, now the BendTec pipe fabrication plant. The boiler is upside down; it would normally sit on the steel pads shown. The furnaces that burned the coal fuel are on the other side of the boiler. The ends of the stay bolts used to restrain the flat heads from internal boiler pressure protrude from the back. Source: Author's collection.

power plant. A study of the machinery for these steamships demonstrates that the company was capable of developing state-of-the-art designs including a forced draft boiler installation for the *City of Everett*, a six-boiler 3,000 hp power plant for the *Christopher Columbus*, and a water-tube boiler quadruple expansion engine installation for the *Alexander McDougall*.[20]

All whaleback steamships were propelled by reciprocating steam engines, the only method for mechanically propelling a ship in the 1890s. The other marine propulsion systems common in the twentieth century—the steam turbine or the internal combustion (diesel) engine—were not yet available for commercial use. The reciprocating steam engine was ideal for Great Lakes ships. It could drive slow-turning propellers without reduction gearing, it was easily reversible for maneuvering, and it could be built in the machine shops around the lakes. The first whalebacks were powered by compound engines (two cylinders sequentially expanding the steam). By the time the whaleback steamships *A. D. Thompson* and *E. B. Bartlett* were launched in 1891, triple expansion engines (three cylinders sequentially expanding the steam) were used. The last whaleback ship built in 1898, the *Alexander McDougall*, was fitted with a quadruple expansion engine.[21]

Power plant efficiency is increased by condensing the steam back to water after it has been expanded in the engine. This allows more of the energy contained in the steam to be turned into useful work. In the 1890s two types of condensers were used for this purpose: jet condensers and surface condensers. Jet condensers mix cold lake water directly with the exhaust steam to condense it. Jet condensers were compact, simple, and cheap and were used in whaleback ships designed for freshwater service.

Surface condensers are boxes honeycombed with many small tubes to maximize the surface area over which heat transfer occurs. Cold lake or sea water passes through the tubes, condensing the steam exhausting from the engine, which flows around the outside of the tubes. The condensing steam is therefore isolated from the cooling water. These were more expensive and difficult to build and could be fouled by the primitive lubricants used in engine cylinders, but they were required for all of the whaleback steamships intended for ocean service as the fresh water feeding the boilers could not be mixed with salt water.[22]

Lighting on earlier ships was provided by oil lamps and skylights. McDougall's patented skylight continued to be used, and a number of these patented skylights have been found on the SS *Meteor*, launched in 1896 as the *Frank Rockefeller*, and

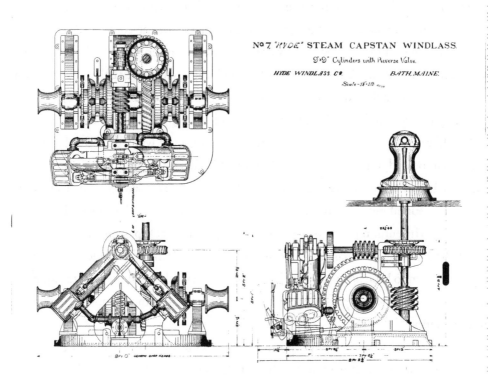

A drawing of the windlass housed in the forward turret of the whaleback steamship *Frank Rockefeller*, which was typical of the steam-powered machinery used aboard whaleback barges and steamships. The two hourglass-shaped drums visible in the top view protruded from the sides of the turret and were used to cat the anchors (hoist them into their stowage position after they had been raised from the bottom). The vertical capstan sat atop the turret; it was driven by a worm gear and was used to handle hemp mooring cables.

now the world's only remaining whaleback steamship.[23] The package freighters *Washburn* and *Pillsbury*, built in 1892, and the passenger steamship *Christopher Columbus*, launched in 1893, were the first whaleback ships to be fitted with electric generating sets.[24] Electricity was used for lighting only. All auxiliary machinery such as capstans for handling mooring lines and windlasses for handling the anchors were powered by steam as compact electric motors were not yet available for this machinery to be electrified.

McDougall's enthusiasm for his whaleback concept was unbounded, and he appears to have been a firm believer in the old adage "it pays to advertise." To do this he made full use of the limited technology of the day. Well-known photographer David F. Barry was hired to document construction of these vessels, and two leading Great Lakes ship portrait painters, Howard Sprague and Vincent Nickerson, traveled from Cleveland to paint portraits of whaleback ships (real and imaginary) for the company.[25]

Ship models and full-sized ships were also used as promotional tools. *Marine Review* reported that the American Steel Barge Company exhibit at the 1893 Columbian Exposition included models of the passenger steamer *Christopher Columbus*, a bulk cargo vessel similar to the *Colgate Hoyt*, and a barge similar to *Barge 102*.[26]

In addition to photographs and paintings, two very old whaleback display models have been located. One model, owned by the Mariners Museum in Newport News, Virginia, is either the whaleback steamship *Frank Rockefeller*, launched in 1896, or an earlier conceptual representation of this vessel. The second model, owned by Duluth Children's Museum, represents a proposed large whaleback passenger vessel (but it is not the famous and smaller *Christopher Columbus*). Unlike the crude experimental models known to have been made by McDougall, the workmanship of these two models is of high quality. It is possible they were built for the specific purpose of exposition and marketing.[27]

McDougall was constantly proposing new variations to the original bulk carrier design. Two of his ideas were to use his whaleback vessels for coastal defense ships and as transatlantic passenger steamers. Although these two ideas died on the drawing board, his efforts did result in construction of several unique whaleback barges and steamships during this period.

On Saturday, June 25, 1892, the company celebrated a "triple launch" of the two whaleback steamships *Washburn* and *Pillsbury* and the yard tug *Islay*.[28] With an overall length of 320 ft., a molded beam of 42 ft., and molded depth of 25.5 ft., these two steamships were the largest whaleback vessels built to date.[29] Both were built for a subsidiary of the Soo Line Railroad for the package freight trade. Package freight was the Great Lakes term for general cargo: bagged flour, hardware, canned food, and so forth. It was carried in boxes and barrels, and to facilitate loading and unloading, these ships were fitted with large gangways cut into the side of the hull. Because package freight cargos would be damaged if stacked too high, the ships also had an intermediate "tween deck."

Marine Review reported that American Steel Barge's contract required that each of the two vessels must be able to carry 3,000 tons of package freight. Because the ships were unable to do so, the Soo Line's steamship company filed suit in Duluth to assess a penalty of $1.00 per ton per year for each ton that the ships could not carry.[30] At

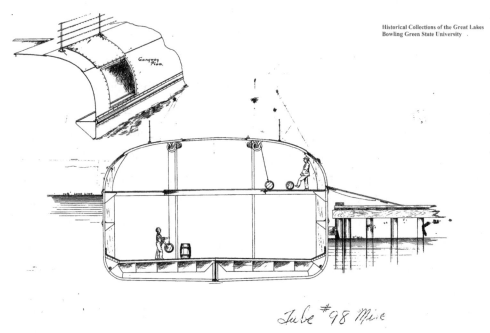

Jube #98 Mine

A cross-sectional view of a whaleback barge or steamship fitted to haul package freight, in this case probably flour in barrels. Cargo is loaded through gangways in the side of the vessel and is stowed on two levels. The upper deck, known as a "tween deck," would not be present on vessels designed for bulk cargo trades. A system of overhead pulleys on a common steam-driven shaft was used to lower cargo to the hold below. Source: Bowling Green State University Special Collections-Entry 988.

their board meetings during the winter of 1893, the American Steel Barge Company's directors treated this problem as an opportunity. They were willing to build two larger steamships for the Soo Line and to add the *Washburn* and the *Pillsbury* to the American Steel Barge fleet.[31] In any event, the Soo Line did not allow the American Steel Barge Company to build two larger steamships, and the problem was not resolved until the deficient vessels were finally added to John D. Rockefeller's newly established Bessemer Steamship Company's fleet in 1896.[32]

It is hard to understand how an experienced shipmaster like McDougall would fail to realize that vessels with the whaleback hull form would be poorly suited for the package freight trades. Naval architects V. N. Minorsky and R. J. Tapscott explained:

> One of the principal factors conducive to profitable operation in the long run is the operator's ability to make his ships "full and down."
>
>   This means that the ship is down to her marks (Plimsoll) with all cargo

cubic fully occupied. It is not the ability to obtain cargo for the vessel which is involved. "Full and down" operation implies that the basic cargo-carrying characteristics of the ship are suited to her particular trade.[33]

For each commodity, there is a "stowage factor" that lists the cubic feet occupied by one ton of cargo. The smaller the stowage factor, the heavier the cargo. "Heavy" cargos, referred to as displacement cargos, weigh a ship down without filling it up. "Light" cargos, referred to as measurement cargos, fill the ship up without weighing it down. In Britain, the dividing line between displacement and measurement cargos was fixed at 40 cu. ft./ton. Table 6 provides stowage factors for different commodities. The trick for the naval architect, when designing a ship to haul a light cargo, is to make full use of the ship's displacement (cargo floating capacity) when her holds are completely filled. A ship's displacement is determined by underwater dimensions and constrained by hull shape and environmental factors such as depth of channel and lock dimensions. A ship designed to haul light cargo needs an underwater volume only large enough to float its cargo and ensure adequate transverse and longitudinal stability, and a large above-water volume to stow bulky goods. Period illustrations of Great Lakes package freighters show that they typically had oversized (by bulk freighter standards) super-structures. Alternatively, a very heavy cargo will weigh the ship down to its desired draft without completely filling its underwater volume; its hull above water needs only be large enough to provide reserve buoyancy required for safety.

The idea behind the whaleback ship was to provide maximum displacement (underwater volume to float cargo) and minimum above-water volume to save cost and weight. Since package freight is a light cargo, the whalebacks' small volume above water would have prevented them from hauling enough cargo to make them "full and down."

The inboard profile drawing for the *Washburn* and the *Pillsbury* shows cubic capacities for each of the ships' four lower cargo holds as well as the single upper cargo hold above the tween deck. This drawing also shows weight of cargo carried at different drafts as well as bunker weights.[34]

McDougall's notebook shows that contract draft for these vessels was 17 ft. At a draft of 17 ft., each ship could float 3,539 tons of "heavy" cargo, well over the 3,000 ton specification requirement. For "light" cargos, a different picture emerges. According to the American Steel Barge Company drawing, the hold capacity volume was 155,116 cu. ft.[35]

Dividing this cubic capacity of the hold by the specified cargo weight of 3,000 tons yields a stowage factor of 51.7 cu. ft./ton. In other words, 3,000 tons of cargo with a stowage factor larger than 51.7 cu. ft./ton would not fit aboard these ships.

Stowage factors listed in table 6 show that these ships could almost load a full cargo of bagged wheat, but only 2,585 tons of flour—well short of the 3,000 ton requirement. The drawing notes that these hold capacities are measured to the "skin of the ship," ignoring the existence of a grid of hull frames and deep web frames within the cargo holds. If the hold cubage is calculated to the inside of this structural grid, the ships could not load a full cargo of freight if the stowage factor exceeded 46 cu. ft./ton, thus excluding all package freight commodities.

Table 6: Stowage Factors	
Commodity	Factor (cu. ft./ton)
Bulk barley	54
Bagged barely	60
Cases of bacon	64–66
Bagged bran	104–110
Cased or barrels of butter	70
Bulk cargo coal	42–56
Bagged flour	44–50
Flour barrels	60
Bulk iron ore	12–17
Bulk oats	76
Bagged oats	83
Pig iron	10
Bulk wheat	47
Bagged wheat	52

Sources: George Simpson, *The Naval Constructor* (London: Van Nostrand, 1918), 771; P. N. Thomas, *British Ocean Tramps*, vols. 1 and 2 (Wolverhampton: Waine Research Publications, 1992), 91.

A two-deck package freighter, stowing cargo on the doublebottom top and tween deck, would require some sort of elevator for handling cargo. Some package freighters built during this period were fitted with steam-powered freight elevators for this purpose.[36] An American Steel Barge Company drawing of cargo in barrels being stowed aboard a whaleback package freighter shows a system of pulleys driven by a geared shaft that would have been driven by a steam engine.[37]

American Steel Barge Company correspondence and drawings indicate that *Barges 126* and *127* (which the company intended to own and operate) were also initially fitted for the package trade, in this case flour.[38]

The third ship of this series was the steamer *Pathfinder.* This ship, and its consort barge *Sagamore* (not to be confused with the English whaleback steamship of the same name), were built as conventional bulk freight whalebacks for the Huron Barge Company, a subsidiary of Pickands Mather. They appear to have operated successfully.[39]

With the possible exception of the *Christopher Columbus* (discussed below), the two steamships built for the Soo Line and the steamship and barge consort built for Pickands Mather were the only four whalebacks the American Steel Barge Company was able to sell to an outside customer prior to 1896. In neither case did the company make money building these ships. Only after applying some creative accounting that involved backing out normally accrued costs—use of tools and prorated general expense—did the company eke out the small profit of $13,788 on revenue of $604,500 (slightly in excess of 2%).[40]

With his experience as master of Great Lakes passenger steamers, it is not surprising that on March 23, 1891, Alexander McDougall applied for a patent for a whaleback passenger ship. U.S. Patent 500,411, issued to McDougall on June 27, 1892, described his ideas for such a vessel.[41]

McDougall's idea for a passenger ship utilized a whaleback hull with seven to ten turrets. A long deck spanned these turrets, and McDougall proposed that this deck be reinforced to add to the longitudinal strength of the hull—a concept structurally similar to the Doxford turret ship. Cabins for passenger accommodation were arranged on top of this deck. He also proposed to subdivide the whaleback hull with a series of transverse and longitudinal bulkheads to make the ship, as stated in his patent, "almost unsinkable." McDougall intended that the whaleback hull form be modified to allow twin or even triple screw propulsion.[42]

Like many of his ideas, this proposed passenger ship was an adaptation of designs previously used by others. Passenger steamers in Great Britain featured passenger accommodations built into the ship's hull, but American passenger steamers sailing on protected or semiprotected waters carried passengers on light superstructure decks elevated above the hull, with the hull and the main deck carrying the ship's machinery and sometimes freight. Examples of these ships could be found on the eastern and western rivers and on the Great Lakes.[43] Although it looked very different, McDougall's passenger steamship followed the established American custom—if for no other reason than that the ship's machinery was hot and dirty, and no paying passenger would want to be near it.

Where passengers on traditionally designed American steamships would have gained access to passenger quarters via open stairways running from the main deck to the second deck, the stairways were placed within reinforced turrets. To load passengers aboard the ship, McDougall imitated the gangways of the two package freighters built for the Soo Line by cutting the gangway into the side of the whaleback hull.

Original in its entirety or not, McDougall's design for a passenger steamer was ingenious. The whaleback hull had been found to be easily driven but lacking in the internal volume to stow low-density cargos. Passengers required a lot of space; a 200 lb. man standing on a 3 ft. by 3 ft. area has a stowage factor of 900 cu. ft./ton. Thousands of people could not crowd into the confines of a whaleback hull, but by using the hull to provide flotation and house machinery, McDougall could provide ample passenger space on the decks elevated above.

Approximately eighteen months after applying for his passenger ship patent, McDougall got a chance to test his ideas with a steamship built to ferry passengers a short distance from downtown Chicago to the site of the 1893 Columbian Exposition. A new syndicate, the Columbian Whaleback Steamship Company, was formed to own the ship. In his autobiography McDougall writes that members of the syndicate were the same people "interested with us in the American Steel Barge Company." In addition, the barge company itself promised to commit $90,000 to the project.[44]

This ship, named the *Christopher Columbus*, was launched on December 3, 1892. She was 360 ft. long, with a beam of 42 ft., and a depth of hull of 24 ft. Seven turrets spanned the hull, providing support for the passenger-carrying superstructure and housing stairwells from gangways cut into the hull to the passenger accommodations. She was equipped with an electric lighting plant and powered by a 3,000 hp triple expansion engine supplied with steam from six boilers.[45]

In his history of the Lake Michigan passenger trade, Professor George W. Hilton claims that the *Christopher Columbus* was built to publicize the whaleback concept at the1893 Columbian Exposition: "McDougall was mainly interested in marketing his innovation for the bulk trade, which was expanding rapidly. The fair was an ideal venue for him; it was a comprehensive display of modern technology, such that having a ship of this design be one's entry could only give the impression that whalebacks were state-of-the-art."[46]

This may be true, as the contract with the Columbian Whaleback Steamship Company to build the ship refers to its promotional nature, and its directors were concerned that the ship would not be finished in a manner that would well represent the company. Over McDougall's objections, they even tried to convene a special meeting to approve the ship's interior furnishings.[47] In the end, the ship was described by the *Chicago Tribune* as furnished in lavish style, with "carpets of Wilton velvet, wainscoting, and paneling in carved oak, chairs and lounges of russet Turkish leather; mauve tints predominate in the mural decorations. There are aquariums, paintings, etc. Baths, barber shops, and restaurants have first class fittings and give excellent service."[48]

Considering that the ship's function was to move fairgoers a short distance of less than ten miles from downtown Chicago to the fairground location, it is hard to see how passengers would have had time to enjoy a shave, a haircut, and a good meal. Still, chartered to the World's Fair Steamship Company, the *Christopher Columbus* carried two million passengers during the fair and was considered a success. For a drawing of *Christopher Columbus*, see plate 4.

Whether she was a successful business venture is another matter. As a promotional tool her timing could not have been worse. The Panic of 1893 plunged the country into depression by the time the fair ended in late autumn; nobody was interested in building ships, passenger or otherwise. At a cost of $361,670, she was expensive, and the American Steel Barge Company may have lost money on her construction as they agreed to build her for their actual cost plus 12.5% but not to exceed $300,000.[49] For this same expenditure they could have built five barges or two large bulk carrying steamships. Since her construction was financed by the same investors as the American Steel Barge Company and by the company itself, she siphoned off money that could have been used to stem the company's growing cash flow deficit. Although she was owned by the Columbian Whaleback Steamship Company, the *Columbus* tapped the same financial resources as any other company-owned whaleback vessel.

After the Columbian Exposition closed, the Columbian Whaleback Steamship Company attempted to find a financially stable owner to operate the *Christopher Columbus* in the Chicago to Milwaukee excursion trade. One such venture failed, forcing the Columbian Whaleback Steamship Company to operate her for the 1898 season. She was bought in 1898 or 1899 by investors affiliated with the Goodrich steamship interests who added a third passenger deck in 1900. In 1909 ownership was transferred to the Goodrich Transit Company, and she sailed for this line in the daily Chicago to Milwaukee excursion trade until she was withdrawn from service in 1931.[50]

As a technical accomplishment, the *Christopher Columbus* represented a successful adaptation of the whaleback hull form, and she safely delivered millions of passengers to their destination during her long career. However, she had no influence on the design of subsequent Great Lakes passenger steamships, and her passenger hauling success did not stimulate the purchase of whaleback barges and steamships, passenger carrying or otherwise. She remained a nautical curiosity throughout her long career.

Companies in niche markets diversify to avoid risking entire investments on the success or failure of one venture. The American Steel Barge Company's attempts to introduce whalebacks to saltwater commerce, described in chapter 7, and its construction of unique vessels for the package goods and passenger trades were attempts at diversification—either producing new products or creating new markets for existing products. Unfortunately, both approaches proved unsuccessful for the American Steel Barge Company.

While diversification is usually considered to be a wise business strategy, the company did not have the financial resources for efforts that would not improve its cash position. Events in 1893 would soon prove that the company's diversification plans should have been evaluated more carefully before proceeding.

CHAPTER 9

The Rockefeller Era

As the American Steel Barge Company's heyday year of 1892 drew to a close, the story shifted from people at the operational level running the business, to the action of four top managers who would determine its future.

The first of these was of course Alexander McDougall. As a fixture of Duluth's growing business community, McDougall was familiar with the activities of the Merritt brothers, who had recently discovered huge deposits of easily mined iron ore north of the city on what would come to be known as the Mesabi Range. The Merritts realized that the ore was valueless unless it could be economically shipped to the steel mills, and this required a railroad from the mines to Lake Superior. Such a railroad already existed to haul ore from underground mines near Ely to the docks at Two Harbors, Minnesota. The Merritts, wishing to control their own destiny and costs, decided to build a completely new railroad to connect with new ore docks that they intended to build at Duluth. In trying to do so they had run out of money and were in danger of defaulting on construction contracts.[1]

Believing that his financial partners in the American Steel Barge Company had access to vast sums of money, McDougall offered to introduce the Merritt brothers to these eastern capitalists in exchange for a contract giving the barge company the right to ship the output of the Mesabi Range down the lakes from Duluth at prevailing rates.[2] While McDougall had many impractical ideas, this was most certainly not one of them. When the Merritts had finished their railroad and ore loading dock, the exclusive right to haul their cargo would have solved the company's most pressing problem—keeping their ships moving with profitable cargos. Whether his partners actually controlled enough capital to meet the Merritts' needs remained to be seen.

C. W. Wetmore

A portrait of Charles W. Wetmore, lawyer, financier, American Steel Barge Company officer and board member, whose financial machinations embroiled the barge company in a dispute and lawsuit with Duluth's Merritt brothers, discoverers of the Mesabi Iron Range.

The second important player was McDougall's contact for the Merritts' financing—Charles W. Wetmore, the barge company's second vice president. He seems to have been the investors' principal contact with the company; he made multiple visits to the West Superior yard and had detailed opinions on its management. Wetmore was born in Hinckley, Ohio, in rural Medina County south of Cleveland. His family later moved to Marquette, Michigan, where he grew up. He graduated from Harvard Law School, was well known in New York yacht racing circles, and in 1891 married author Elizabeth Bisland. In the fall of 1892 he was thirty-eight years old.[3]

Unfortunately for the company's future, Wetmore was highly leveraged, using shares of companies that he had previously invested in as marketable collateral to borrow ever more cash for new ventures. In the fall of 1892 he made a trip to northern Wisconsin and Minnesota with English ship owner William Johnston. He also visited the Merritt brothers' newly developed iron ore properties and discussed financing.[4] In his detailed report of the trip, he proposed that Hoyt raise an additional $1,000,000 for the barge company and ended with the following optimistic statement: "I am strongly impressed with the feeling that in the Lake Country alone there is ample opportunity for the profitable investment of all the money that we can reasonably hope to command, and that with every additional dollar invested will come greater certainty of increased profits from the investments already made."[5]

The third key player was company president Colgate Hoyt, who unfortunately had little influence on the upcoming events because he was sick, suffering from what McDougall said was typhoid fever.[6] In the fall of 1892 Hoyt was preparing to travel to

Europe to take the cure, as such treatment and recuperation was called. Nevertheless, before leaving, he responded to Wetmore's optimism with a letter that demonstrated his remarkable ability to understand the economic forces affecting the company and to clearly communicate the effect of these forces on its business strategy. Hoyt wrote:

> I approve the lines you are now working on namely, in securing if possible capitalists among our friends to furnish the money to complete this railroad ... but I am utterly opposed to the barge company making any subscription or taking any interest itself in the building of railroads or the purchase of iron ore mines. We must be very careful of entangling alliances. We are a construction and transportation company and in our desire to get more business we must not be led into the construction of railroads, or the purchase of iron mines, flour mills or any other branches of business. If we do this, in my judgment sooner or later we will heartily regret it.
>
> But you must remember that our friends have large interests in iron ore mines on Lake Superior, Mr. Rockefeller especially, in the Minnesota Iron Company as well in our Gogebic mines and we must not do anything without his full knowledge and concent [sic] which in any way might be considered prejudicial to his interests.
>
> I would make no Department independent of Captain McDougall. While I would relieve him of all detail work as much as possible, I would on no account have any Department feel that they have any communication with the New York office, except through Captain McDougall as General Manager. My faith in him as an inventor and as a constructor and practical manager is greater than ever and while I know it is a fact that he has had more on his shoulders during the past year and that he can be relieved of much of the detail work that he has had to do in the past still in the organization of work in the departments I would be very careful to see that all orders to such heads of Departments come through Captain McDougall and that all reports sent from these Departments direct to the New York office be sent only on his orders as General Manager.
>
> I know both you and he (Bartlett) will agree most heartily with me in my suggestions as to the importance of our continuing the centralization of power through our General Manager.

I cannot but feel that with the change in administration of the government, with the certain tendency towards a lower tariff and a probability of the duty being removed on raw material bringing with these changes cheaper labor—with the financial complications growing out of the silver problem that within the next eighteen months this country is going to see a decided setback in all new enterprises, and that we will have a period of business stagnation. I therefore suggest that we do not immediately commit ourselves to any additional construction until it is finally decided as to whether we are going to have two more steamers to build for the Canadian Pacific Railroad (vessels with greater carrying capacity to replace the whalebacks *Washburn* and *Pillsbury*) and no matter what temptation may be do not get ourselves committed to any sum beyond what we have already secured cash for.

I know the "Captain's" marvelous energy and ability to grind out work, but he had too much for any one man to do last year and I beg of you gentlemen on the Executive Committee to hold him back and not let him have such a strain again during the coming year or he will find himself before he knows it, on the shelf where I am now, and we can't any of us afford that.

I have simply written these notes to you as suggestions, knowing that you will all of you come to wise conclusions in these matters.[7]

The paragraphs in Hoyt's letter regarding McDougall's status are curious. Accompanying Wetmore on his fall 1892 trip to West Superior was E. B. Bartlett, one of the company's original directors.[8] Based on comments in Wetmore's trip report, Bartlett must have been an accountant. Perhaps in today's business jargon he would have been the company's chief financial officer (CFO). In this report, Wetmore revealed that discussions were taking place to relieve McDougall of his day-to-day shipyard management responsibilities and to place Joseph Kidd in charge of yard operations. Furthermore, Kidd would report to New York, bypassing McDougall through a reporting system to be devised by Bartlett. The reasons for this were not explained, and Wetmore claimed that McDougall agreed with the change. Wetmore then stated in his report that: "there was very little to criticize in the local management, either of the ship building plant or of the transportation business. Naturally with a man at the head of affairs, possessing so much energy as Captain McDougall, we find corresponding energy and activity among the heads of departments and employees of the company."[9]

Less complimentary was Wetmore's impression of Kidd:

> Mr. Kidd is a very quiet man, in regard to whom it is difficult to judge, and I do not place much confidence in my own first impressions as to the character and capacity of men. From my personal observation however I do not yet feel satisfied that he is entirely competent for a place of much responsibility, but this cannot be decided for some time, as Captain McDougall has never heretofore left him in full charge. The results of this winter's operations will probably show whether he possesses the requisite ability.[10]

This entire discussion, therefore, seems more about removing McDougall from his hands-on management position than about promoting Kidd to improve operations. Perhaps the New York management team wanted to increase their control, perhaps Wetmore and/or Bartlett did not get along with the rough-hewn McDougall, or—unlikely as it may seem—McDougall himself might have been bored with the day-to-day management of the yard and was anxious to have more time to devote to promoting his whaleback ships. This is all speculation, and the existing documentation does not provide an answer.

The last of the key players in the events of late 1892 through early 1893 was an unlikely one. John D. Rockefeller had hired Frederick Gates, a Baptist minister, to organize and evaluate the many requests for charitable donations he received as a result of his tremendous wealth. Gates demonstrated a remarkable ability to understand financial matters, so Rockefeller asked him to look into the investments sold to him by Colgate Hoyt and others. While Gates may have been a financial whiz, he seems to have been burdened with a self-righteous and disagreeable personality that interfered with his ability to work with entrepreneurs like Alexander McDougall.[11]

Gates made a trip to Superior, Wisconsin, in August 1892 to check on the West Superior Iron and Steel Company. He claims that the company was nothing more than a front intended to show activity indicating an economic boom in the town to promote real estate sales. Gates does not mention American Steel Barge Company in his autobiography, yet he must have visited it at this same time. He would have learned

Frederick T. Gates, Baptist minister hired by John D. Rockefeller to evaluate charitable requests and later to manage his many outside investments. Following Rockefeller's recapitalization of the American Steel Barge Company in the fall of 1892, Gates became its de facto head. He streamlined the company's operations to allow it to better compete in the climate that existed after the Panic of 1893, but in doing so alienated Colgate Hoyt and ultimately Alexander McDougall.

that while operation of the barge and steamship fleet was producing an operational profit, matters at the corporate level were less positive. In late 1892 the business was short of cash. On September 15, 1892, the company forecasted cash requirements through year-end of $823,000, with available resources of only $787,708, for a cash shortfall of $35,291.[12] Just six weeks later the shortfall had grown to $124,826, and this assumed that $400,000 in new capital could be raised.[13] Several factors had caused this problem:

1. As noted earlier, the cash flow problem revealed a flawed business strategy. The company owned a shipyard dedicated to production of one type of vessel—whalebacks—and a steamship line that operated those ships. By failing to gain market approval for their whaleback ships, the yard had only one steady customer for its vessels—its own steamship line. If the yard was to keep busy, it had to produce and to finance an ever-growing fleet of vessels for the steamship line, whether they were needed or not. This resulted in a constant and growing need for cash.

2. The passenger steamship *Christopher Columbus* cost $361,670, enough to build five barges or two large whaleback steamships. Instead of selling the ship to someone else and turning over its cash, the company elected (or was forced) to operate the vessel itself, through the new Columbian Whaleback Steamship Company as mentioned earlier.[14]

3. American Steel Barge intended to loan money to four unspecified entities related to the investors for a total of $95,000.[15]

4. The company intended to pay out $400,000 in cash dividends.[16]

Not included in these estimates was Wetmore's ambitious proposal to build four additional barges and one steamship during the winter of 1892–1893 at an additional cost of over $400,000.[17]

On December 14, 1892, before leaving for Europe, Colgate Hoyt attempted to meet the company's cash needs by sending a letter to all shareholders allowing them to buy additional shares of stock. The total amount to be subscribed was $1,000,000, and shareholders could purchase the new shares pro rata based on shares that they already owned.[18] When this failed to produce the desired results, Hoyt turned to the one investor who had the resources to save the company: John D. Rockefeller. Beginning with an initially modest $15,000, Rockefeller's investment in the company had grown to a substantial sum that he apparently felt was too large to lose.[19] In the absence of other investors willing to participate, Rockefeller agreed to a first mortgage of up to $4,000,000 secured by all of the company's assets: their shipyard, ships, and intangible property including McDougall's patents. The company even pledged steamships and barges to be built in the future. The mortgage was held by the Rockefeller-controlled Farmers Bank. Although it was recorded on June 6, 1893, it had been in effect since January 1.[20] As early as December 1892, several days before the mortgage took effect, Duluth newspapers were boasting that the American Steel Barge Company was backed by John D. Rockefeller and his wealth.[21]

Rockefeller would have preferred a mortgage to a stock purchase for two reasons. First, in the event of a bankruptcy, a mortgage would place Rockefeller "first in line" as the collateral assets securing the mortgage would be sold off to satisfy the debt ahead of other less-secured creditors. Stockholders would only be paid off if and when all debts had been satisfied. Second, if Rockefeller was to provide financing he wanted control of the company. Because he was a minority shareholder, there was a real risk that the majority shareholders who controlled the board might issue shares of "watered stock," diluting his interests. With a mortgage, he could provide restrictive loan covenants that would allow him a hand in the company's management and protect him as a minority shareholder from stock manipulations.[22]

Rockefeller's refinancing of the American Steel Barge Company was typical of other situations in which he was trying to recoup his investments in troubled companies. In an article about Rockefeller's western mining properties, Colorado Historical Society author James E. Fell Jr. describes the process:

> This pattern repeated itself many times over the next few years: a request for the oil magnate's money to continue development, a denial from Gates unless others would invest their share, and finally an infusion of Rockefeller capital when other shareholders either would not or could not advance more funds.
>
> Yet in each case Gates was careful to acquire securities in the mining firms as collateral and to make the loans through the Everett & Monte Cristo Railway, which he served as president and which Rockefeller controlled.[23]

Rockefeller's dealings with the American Steel Barge Company followed this pattern, with Rockefeller issuing a mortgage, secured by the company's assets, through a bank that he controlled.

In the first two months of 1893 while Colgate Hoyt was in Europe, the company's board of directors, ignoring his sage advice, took advantage of this newfound source of cash and unanimously decided to build not four but six new barges as well as one steamship. The barges, numbered 129 through 134, would be launched in May and June 1893.[24] Construction of the steamship would be delayed by upcoming events for two years.[25] The board also approved a proposed contract with the Merritts to haul ore from their newly developed Mesabi Range mines for fifteen years, as well as the Wetmore/Bartlett proposal to place Joseph Kidd in day-to-day charge of the shipyard. McDougall remained general manager, and it is not known if Wetmore's idea to by-pass McDougall was implemented.[26]

Sometime in early 1893 (probably March) Frederick Gates arrived in Duluth to represent Rockefeller and in effect to become the company's chief executive officer.[27]

One of Gates's first actions was to cancel the contract with the Merritts to haul their Mesabi Range ore. McDougall was outraged, and this does appear to have been a foolish decision.[28] There are two possible reasons, however, why Gates might have decided to do this.

1. Gates may have wanted to avoid committing the vessels of the whaleback fleet to a yet unproven mining venture, thereby eliminating the need to continue building additional ships. McDougall stated that in the spring of 1893 Gates had not been able to sell the Mesabi ores, so "there was nothing for the barge company to carry."[29] Steel industry historians have explained that it took a while for blast furnace operators, who were used to smelting the hard rock ores, to learn how to smelt the soft powdery hematite ores of the Mesabi Range.[30]

2. Another possible reason for cancellation of the contract may have been to avoid wedding the production of the mines to the cost structure of the whaleback fleet. Transportation costs were an ongoing thread of John D. Rockefeller's business life. His domination of the eastern oil business had been achieved by controlling the rail lines from the Pennsylvania oil fields.[31] In the 1890s, Great Lakes ship design was rapidly evolving and there was no

way to tell if whaleback ships would still be viable at the end of the period. (As it turned out whaleback ships were still hauling ore fifteen years later, but they had been eclipsed by much larger vessels of more conventional design.) Even so, it is hard to understand why Gates did not try to leave the contract in place, perhaps reducing risk by shortening its duration.

All in all, whether due to problems with the Mesabi ores or bad economic conditions in general, cancellation of the Merritt ore hauling contract appears irrational 130 years later. Great Lakes steamship operators understood how to book short-term contracts and how to lay ships up to minimize costs when cargos were not available. It appears there would have been no cost to the company to have let the contract stand as long as it did not stimulate the construction of additional unneeded ships. It is hard to disagree with McDougall that Gates's first decision was unwise.

Colgate Hoyt's refinancing of the company in the late fall of 1892 had happened none too soon. By early 1893 events began to indicate that the financial crisis that he had predicted would occur. Collapse of the Philadelphia and Reading Railroad in late February and the National Cordage Company in April triggered a selloff of stocks in May by panicky investors concerned that their holdings were greatly overvalued. As the crisis cascaded through the economy, banks restricted credit and called in loans. The resulting depression that lasted through 1894 and 1895 caused a reduction in business activity, including the need for transportation services.[32] Wild rates for shipments of iron ore from Lake Superior to Lake Erie ports fell from $1.13 per ton to $0.77 per ton, a drop of almost 32%.[33]

The American Steel Barge Company responded to the economic crisis in the way that shipbuilders and ship owners always do—they hunkered down to weather the storm. Construction of whaleback vessels at the West Superior yard was drastically curtailed. The six barges that had been authorized before the panic were completed in the spring of 1893, and two oil barges were built for Rockefeller's Standard Oil Company. Although there are drawings for whaleback tank barges in the American Steel Barge Company archives and many whaleback barges sailed in the East Coast tanker trade, these were of conventional design.[34] After that, no new vessels were laid down until 1896. Work on hull 135, the steamship, later named *John Trevor*, was slowed down and the ship was not launched until May 1, 1895.[35] The whaleback fleet itself would have been laid up and crews laid off when not needed to haul paying cargos, a practice used as recently as the Great Recession of 2009, when idle Great Lakes ships could be found moored in harbors around the lakes, waiting for better times.

After dealing with the immediate crisis caused by the Panic of 1893, Gates could consider the company's long-term future. He would have acted in accordance with Rockefeller's stated business policy:

> It was our policy never to allow a company in which we had an interest
> to be thrown into the bankruptcy court. This was an anathema. Rather it
> was our plan . . . to stay with the institution, nurse it, lend it money where
> necessary, improve facilities, cheapen production, and avail ourselves of the
> opportunities which time and patience (were) likely to bring to make itself
> sustaining and successful.[36]

The subsequent history of the American Steel Barge Company is best understood in light of this business strategy.

While Rockefeller had no desire to lose his investment by liquidating viable companies, like any prudent business owner he spent the succeeding years (through his agent Frederick Gates) shedding unnecessary assets to allow American Steel Barge to focus on its core business interests.

After completing the whaleback steamship *City of Everett* in late 1894, Gates closed the Pacific Steel Barge Company's shipyard at Everett, Washington.[37] As the whaleback ship design had failed to gain acceptance with saltwater shippers, and as the yard was located thousands of miles from sources of supply and from the East Coast financial interests that bought merchant steamships, there appears to have been no reason for the shipyard other than to provide business activity for the town of Everett, so this would seem to be a sensible decision.

Also terminated was the company's Atlantic Service; *Barges 110, 201, 202* and the steamship *Joseph Colby* were returned to the Great Lakes. Records do not indicate how long service was continued beyond 1892, but the *Colby*, temporarily cut in two to allow passage through the St. Lawrence locks, returned to the lakes in 1896. *Barges 201* and *202* apparently also returned at this time; they were lengthened at the West Superior yard for Great Lakes service during the winter of 1896–1897.[38]

As previously described, following closure of the Columbian Exposition in Chicago the Columbian Whaleback Steamship Company attempted to sell the passenger steamship *Christopher Columbus* to a financially viable owner, although this white elephant was not finally unloaded until 1906.[39] The *C. W. Wetmore* had been wrecked in 1892, and the *City of Everett* was sold to the American Agricultural Chemical Company to haul phosphate across the Gulf of Mexico for Rockefeller's Standard Oil Company.[40] The ships owned by the American Steel Barge Company were now limited to those working in the Great Lakes bulk trades.

The company's operations were further limited in 1895 by a decision to place all of its barges and steamships under the management of Pickands Mather.[41] This was an attempt to address what the directors had considered to be the company's most pressing problem—the dispatch of its ships to allow the most cargo to be hauled during the short Great Lakes shipping season. Writing almost sixty years later, one Great Lakes vessel operator explained problems that would have been all too familiar to McDougall:

> Whereas the vessels of the larger fleets invariably got several cargos of coal to go up to Lake Superior, the Str. *Capt. John Roen* never got one and had to run upbound light. Naturally, what coal became available went to the Companies' own vessels rather than ours. Also at the destination we always got the slowest docks, and the furthest up the river, and the most expensive to get to on account of assisting tug charges.[42]

Pickands Mather was a minor investor in the American Steel Barge Company, and it managed one of the largest fleets on the lakes. It also owned iron mines, so it had its own ore to transport. Its Huron Transportation subsidiary already operated the whaleback barge *Sagamore* and whaleback steamship *Pathfinder*. Although he lived in New York, John D. Rockefeller still maintained close ties with the Cleveland, Ohio, business community and knew the principals in the Pickands Mather firm.

Of the four key players named above, the first to be affected by the events of 1893 was Charles W. Wetmore. Following the signing of the shipping contract with the Merritts, Wetmore agreed to personally purchase their railroad bonds with a face value of $2,000,000 for $1,600,000. He planned to resell these at a profit to associates in the New York financial market. The agreement required Wetmore to pay the Merritts $50,000 upon signing the contract and an additional $450,000 within sixty days.[43] After initially selling some of these bonds to John D. Rockefeller and making some payments, Wetmore ran out of willing customers and cash, putting the Merritts in a severe cash bind. At the same time, he further strained his resources trying to buy out one or more of the Merritts' iron range competitors.[44]

In February or March 1893, Wetmore loaned himself $432,575 from the coffers of the American Steel Barge Company to pay the Merritts. Upon his return from Europe in April 1893, Colgate Hoyt demanded security for this raid on the company's treasury, and Wetmore provided promissory notes from the Merritts and stock in their railroad as collateral.[45] The barge company eventually auctioned off this collateral, resulting in a series of protracted lawsuits between the barge company and the Merritt brothers.

Already in trouble, hurt by the May stock market crash, and finding that investors were uninterested in investing in "a small, distant ore railroad," Wetmore apparently moved around the limited money that he did have to keep various northern Wisconsin and Minnesota mining ventures alive. He used mining stocks and bonds as marketable vehicles to raise cash.[46] By the late summer of 1893 he was in deep financial trouble, and by September of the same year he was known to be insolvent.[47] Wetmore's financial maneuverings destroyed his reputation with the American Steel Barge Company. Hoyt and Colby protested "that Wetmore's reckless methods have destroyed largely the credit of the Barge Company."[48] By 1894 he had lost his positions as officer and director of the company, but his brother Russell C. Wetmore had been appointed corporate secretary.[49] Wetmore eventually recovered from the panic and was active for a number of years in the development of the electric utility industry.

Colgate Hoyt returned from Europe in April 1893. Alexander McDougall wrote of his return, "When Hoyt came back from Europe and found Gates in his place and learned what his interference had accomplished there was a sharp difference between them and a good deal of feeling arose."[50]

Nevertheless, Hoyt appears to have been active in the management of the company for the next several years, struggling to keep the company solvent in the wake of the business depression caused by the panic.

In October 1893, for example, he communicated with the Merritts regarding an extension in the date for auction of the securities held for Wetmore's $432,500 loan. He wrote that the financial condition of the American Steel Barge Company was "such as to make it absolutely impossible to consent to this extension. We are willing and anxious to oblige you in every reasonable way but are so sorely in need of the money that is due that we cannot grant this request."[51] Somehow the company weathered the storm while the Rockefeller faction slowly gained influence.

By February 1894 both Wetmore and Bartlett had left the board. They were replaced by Franklin Rockefeller and James B. Colgate.[52] Things came to a head for Hoyt in November 1896 when he attempted to bypass Gates while negotiating contracts, and by the middle of January 1897 Gates, representing John D. Rockefeller, was in full control.[53] Despite his disagreements with the Rockefeller faction, Hoyt retained his board position and represented the company in the negotiations leading to its merger into the American Shipbuilding Company in 1899.[54]

In spite of the complaints in his autobiography, written approximately twenty-eight years after the fact, McDougall initially appears to have had a cordial relationship with Frederick Gates. He was appointed vice president of the railroad being built between the Mesabi Range and Duluth by the Merritts, and he claimed that the design of the massive ore loading dock built at Duluth was roughed out on his kitchen table. In November 1896 he was still signing letters as general manager of the American Steel Barge Company.[55] In his autobiography, McDougall says that Gates tried to enlist him in a dispute with Hoyt, but he refused as "Hoyt was my principal and had always been square with me and I couldn't turn my back on him."[56] While the autobiography implies that this happened upon Hoyt's return from Europe in 1893, it almost certainly happened in January 1897 or later when Gates was consolidating Rockefeller's ownership of the company. As a result, after learning that McDougall was not really on his team, Gates demanded that McDougall pay off a loan for stock being held in his name.

To raise the necessary cash McDougall had to sell back the stock that he held in the company at what he considered to be unreasonably low prices. In the ongoing negotiations between McDougall and Gates to determine the value of the stock, Gates writes:

> Assets of the company? How much ore carried last year? You will see that what we are getting at is the earning power of the boats, at the present costs which I assume are pretty near the minimum. . . . But, the real point—the point of most vital moment—is what does it actually cost this fleet per ton this year to carry iron ore.[57]

Gates makes two interesting points here. First, he is reminding McDougall that after 1893 the American Steel Barge Company had no unencumbered assets. They had all been pledged to a Rockefeller-controlled bank. The company's sole value lay in the earning potential of its vessels, not the value of the vessels themselves—a remarkably modern way for the time of valuing a company's assets. His second point is that the fleet of small vessels was becoming obsolete in the face of competition from the new, larger ships. McDougall of course did not agree. He says "Worse than that, by Gates' blundering the stock that had been worth double par was knocked down to fifty cents on the dollar."[58] McDougall had bought the stock and had financed the purchase with a loan from the company, so by taking back the stock Gates would have written off half of McDougall's loan. Since it is possible that no actual money ever changed hands, Gates was probably just happy to add McDougall's stock to Rockefeller's holdings and to be done with things.

Rockefeller's takeover and subsequent management of the American Steel Barge Company was controversial. In his autobiography, McDougall complained of Gates's lack of vision, and over the years John D. Rockefeller has acquired the reputation of a greedy takeover artist. The evidence found in my research efforts does not support these assertions. First of all, the company's strategy of continuously building ships required a corresponding increase in capital, and by 1893 the only investor willing and able to provide it was Rockefeller. In addition, in early 1893 the company's directors (including McDougall) ignored Colgate Hoyt's wise council and continued with ill-advised expansion projects, further increasing the need for scarce capital. The actions taken by Rockefeller and Gates reflected a desire to run the company as a going concern. When the downturn resulting from the Panic of 1893 ended, having closed non-core businesses and placed the management of the company's Great Lakes fleet in the hands of professional managers separate from the shipbuilding business, Gates and Rockefeller had put the company in a better position to compete. Gates would continue to loyally serve John D. Rockefeller until 1923. He died in February 1929.[59]

The Hoyt Syndicate's loss of control of the company to John D. Rockefeller was not caused by the Panic of 1893. Frederick Gates's first visit to the company and the Farmers Bank loan that mortgaged its assets occurred eight months and six months, respectively, prior to the May 1893 onset of the panic. Specifically, the need to raise cash in the fall of 1892 occurred as a result of the company's flawed strategy of continuous expansion. But although Rockefeller controlled the company's assets through his mortgage, he did not in 1893 own a controlling interest of the company's stock. The May 1893 stock market crash and the hard times that followed did make it easier for Rockefeller to eventually own the company by acquiring blocks of stock from members of the syndicate hurt by the economic crisis.

CHAPTER 10

The Final Ships

With an unexpected surge in ore shipments during the summer of 1895, optimism returned to the Great Lakes. As a result of his investments on Minnesota's Mesabi Range, John D. Rockefeller had become a major producer of iron ore, but in 1895 he could not charter the shipping necessary to deliver it to lower lakes markets. Rockefeller vowed that he would not be caught in this position again and decided to build his own fleet of ships. To accomplish this he founded the Bessemer Steamship Company.[1] If he regretted Frederick Gates's decision to cancel McDougall's shipping deal with the Merritts, it has not been recorded.

To manage the acquisition and construction of this new fleet he hired Pickands Mather as his agent to contract with Great Lakes yards to build the first twelve vessels. Reflecting the ever-growing size of ships built for the Great Lakes iron ore trade, Pickands Mather specified vessels with an overall length of 400 ft. Two of these, the steamship *John Ericsson* and the consort barge *Alexander Holley*, were awarded to the American Steel Barge Company. Of the twelve vessels ordered, these were the only two of whaleback design. The other ten ships built elsewhere on the lakes were of conventional design.[2]

Building new ships for his fleet would take time, so Rockefeller also bought four whaleback ships that were available. Two of these were the problematic steamships *Washburn* and *Pillsbury*, which had been built for the Soo Line Railroad. Renamed *James B. Neilson* and *Henry Cort*, respectively, and placed in the iron ore trade for which they were better suited, they would work for Bessemer and its successor, the Pittsburgh Steamship Company, for the next thirty years. The other two whaleback vessels acquired in 1896 were barges. *Barge 102* and *Barge 103* were purchased for the Bessemer fleet from the American Steel Barge Company and renamed *Sir Joseph Whitworth* and *John Scott Russell*.[3]

Rockefeller's new Bessemer fleet changed the rules for the American Steel Barge Company. Prior to the Panic of 1893, the company's fleet had been a tramp operation, a saltwater term for securing cargo from many shippers and delivering in accordance with a negotiated contract or the terms of each voyage's charter agreement. Shipping rates and extra expenses that could be charged were set by the market and established Great Lakes custom. Iron ore was unloaded by a stevedoring operation that charged the vessel a fixed rate per ton of cargo regardless of the time needed to unload it.

Rockefeller's Bessemer Steamship Company, however, was part of a transportation system dedicated to delivering ore from his mines to customers at the lowest possible cost. Rockefeller's people could be expected to scrutinize any activities that would affect the delivered cost of his ore.[4] For example, while the American Steel Barge Company routinely tried to increase revenues by hauling coal back up the lakes, ships of several of the larger fleets dedicated to the iron ore trade traveled up-bound in ballast to avoid the time required to load and unload this secondary cargo.[5] Rockefeller's establishment of the Bessemer fleet meant that new whaleback ships added to his fleet would have to compete head-to-head with vessels of conventional design.

As 1895 came to a close, the *John Ericsson* and the *Alexander Holley* were not the only vessels on American Steel Barge Company's books. Earlier in October, the board had authorized construction of another steamship and barge combination to be added to the American Steel Barge fleet. The steamship, hull 136, would be named *Frank Rockefeller*, in honor of John D. Rockefeller's brother, who had been appointed to the company's board in 1894. Following standard company practice, the consort barge was simply named *Barge 137*.[6]

McDougall and his two friends on the board, Thomas Wilson and A. D. Thompson, objected to building these new ships.[7] While their reasoning is not recorded, they might have objected to their large size. At 2,759 gross tons, the *Frank Rockefeller* was 15% larger than the *John Trevor*, the last ship laid down prior to the panic. A comparison of vessel designs probably prepared by McDougall in 1895 or 1896 includes a paragraph which states,

> These boats [small whalebacks such as *Barges 115* and *116*] are small and much more easily handled and require much less dock room. Vessels of

this kind are better adapted for the trade in the lake country, besides being able to go through the Welland Canal, much more convenient in Chicago Harbor and should they be taken to sea in future would be adapted for coastwise trade. *They will show the best results of any* (emphasis in original).[8]

McDougall may have also realized that as Great Lakes vessels became longer the whaleback's structurally weak hull form placed it at an ever-growing disadvantage—it was much more difficult to design the required longitudinal strength into a 400 ft. hull than into a 240 ft. hull.[9] If McDougall truly considered shorter ships to be the wave of the future, he was wasting his time. With the discovery of the huge iron ore deposits on the Mesabi Range, there was a constant need to carry more cargo per trip. With their width and depth limited by the restricted shipping channels of the rivers and harbors of the Great Lakes, ships had to get longer to haul more cargo.

The characteristics of the three new steamships and representative conventional ships are tabulated in table 7.

The first of the new whaleback vessels to be completed was the *Frank Rockefeller*, launched on April 23, 1896. The launch was witnessed by a large crowd and was considered to be sufficiently important to merit a description of the ship in the *Journal of the American Society of Naval Engineers*.[10]

> The hull departs somewhat in appearance from the other whaleback steamers. The deck has less crown and the topsides are straighter. The pilothouse is separate from the main cabins, the intervening space of 34 feet being occupied by fueling hatches. The old plan of placing engines and stacks in separate tunnels (turrets) has been abandoned, and one large turret protects the whole of the space. This greatly improves the ventilation of both the engine and fire rooms. The boilers are placed higher than has heretofore been the practice affording additional cargo space. There are eleven center line cargo hatches, each 12 ft. × 8 ft. And ten side hatches, 6 ft. × 4 ft., the latter located upon the port side of the ship, this arrangement allowing 21 ore spouts to be lowered into the vessel at one time, thereby reducing the time for loading.[11]

The flatter deck mentioned above was a consequence of wider beam. The side hatches were an experiment to increase the number of hatches. The staggered arrange-

Table 7: Characteristics of Late Whaleback Ships

Hull #	Name	Length	Beam	Depth	Gross Tonnage	Displ @ 14 ft. wl.	Cargo @ 14 Ft. wl.	Displ @ 18 ft. wl.	Cargo @ 18 ft. wl.	Cost	$/Ton of Cargo 14 ft. wl.	$/Ton of Cargo 18 ft. wl.
135	*John Trevor*	320	38	24	2400	4060	2750	5410	4100	118,250	43	21.86
136	*Frank Rockefeller*	380	45	26	2759	5690	3367	7523	5200	181,573	53.93	24.14
138	*John Ericsson*	404	48	27	3200	6120	3580	8760	6220	209,334	58.47	23.9
141	*Alexander McDougall*	414	50	27	3686	7650	5150	9975	7475	202,625	39.34	20.31
	Victory (conventional ship, 1895)	398	48	28	3774		4058		5824			
	Mauna Loa	450	50	28.5	4951			10728	7528			

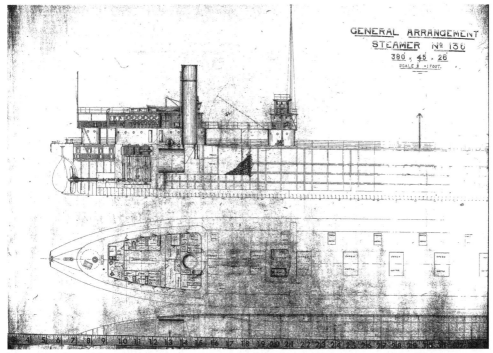

The aft section of the whaleback steamship *Frank Rockefeller*, now the museum ship *Meteor*, showing a number of features incorporated by naval architect A. C. Diericx in the third-generation whaleback vessels. The pilothouse has been moved forward onto a new turret. The coal bunker is placed between this new turret and the after turret, which is elongated to contain both the boiler uptakes and the open space over the engine. The vessel's three boilers have been placed on an elevated deck, making room for a cargo hold below, which is accessed through a cargo trunk passing through the coal bunkers. This awkward hold was apparently an attempt to increase the vessel's cubic cargo capacity. Source: Bowling Green State University Special Collections-Entry 973.

ment cut hatch spacing in half and allowed hatches to line up with the 12 ft. spacing of the ore loading dock spouts while still maintaining a continuous band of shell plating in a highly stressed area of the hull.[12]

The additional cargo space below the ship's three boilers mentioned in the *American Society for Naval Engineers* article is an interesting detail. As the space was beneath the boilers and behind the coal bunkers, access could only be gained by a vertical cargo trunk passing through the bunkers. Cargo had to be lowered down the trunk and then hauled back into the space. Ore, being a very heavy cargo, would have brought the ship to its full load draft before filling the main hold, making this space unnecessary. The difficulties of moving iron ore from the cargo trunk back under the boilers can only be imagined. This cargo space would have therefore been used to provide extra volume to haul light cargos, probably bagged grain. This odd feature was duplicated on the *John Ericsson* even though the new Bessemer fleet was to be dedicated to the ore trade.[13]

Another departure from the previous generation of whaleback ships was the location of the *Frank Rockefeller*'s pilothouse and coal bunkers. Following the design of the *City of Everett*, the *Frank Rockefeller*'s machinery was rearranged so that the coal bunker, previously outboard of the boilers, was now in an unobstructed area of the hull forward of the after quarters. The pilothouse that was formerly located atop the after quarters was now located on top of a separate turret forward of the bunker and 34 ft. forward of the after house.[14] As these ships grew longer it was likely that the pilothouse needed to be farther forward to improve visibility when conning the ship.

It has always been a challenge for the designers of Great Lakes ships to build adequate longitudinal strength into their long, narrow, shallow hulls, and the builders of whaleback ships were at a particular disadvantage as these vessels approached the 400 ft. mark. Designers of Great Lakes bulk carriers typically located heavy continuous longitudinal strength members outboard of the hatches along the corners between the ships' decks and sides, a location where they could effectively resist bending of the hull in a seaway.[15] With their curved decks, whaleback ships had no such corner to reinforce, and the curved shape of the deck caused longitudinal strength members that had to be located outboard of the hatches closer to the ships neutral axis, limiting their effectiveness. To overcome these problems, large continuous girders were placed beneath the deck just outboard of the hatches. These girders in turn limited the width of the hatches.[16]

Another interesting original feature that can still be seen aboard the SS *Meteor* is the extensive use of bulb angles for structural members such as transverse hull frames. Whaleback barges and steamships were previously constructed from built-up Z-sections made from two angles riveted back-to-back. Bulb angles were a structural shape that provided strength without the cost to rivet two angles together. They were widely used in Europe, but not in the United States.[17]

To propel the ship, to provide electric lighting, and to provide steam for auxiliary equipment, American Steel Barge designed a power plant reflecting conventional Great Lakes marine engineering practice: three Scotch marine boilers supplying steam to a triple expansion engine.[18]

The *Frank Rockefeller* was built to tow a consort barge, and in 1896 the company launched a barge of similar dimensions, named *Barge 137*.[19]

Whaleback steamship *Frank Rockefeller* shortly after launch in April 1896. Although owned by the American Steel Barge Company, this vessel was painted in Pickands Mather's colors—rust-colored hull, white turrets, and an orange stripe that can just be seen around the top of the black smokestack. Source: Superior Public Museums.

Ships of the American Steel Barge Company's fleet were painted with rust red hulls and buff-colored turrets. Cabins were finished in dark wood. Early photographs of the *Frank Rockefeller* show her painted with white turrets. This would have been consistent with the Pickands Mather color scheme.[20]

Also launched in 1896 was the larger whaleback steamship *John Ericsson* and its similarly sized consort barge *Alexander Holley*. Both, as explained above, were built for Rockefeller's new Bessemer fleet. Comparison of drawings shows that with one important exception, the *John Ericsson* was an enlarged *Frank Rockefeller*. She was not simply stretched—the ship was not only longer but also wider and deeper.[21] The additional width would have increased cargo capacity as well as adding hull strength by making room for more material in the critical area of the hull girder outboard of the hatch openings. The additional depth also strengthened the hull by increasing the distance from the hull's neutral axis to key strength elements on the deck and bottom.

The obvious difference in design between the *John Ericsson* and the whaleback ships that preceded her concerned the placement of her pilothouse. For the *John Ericsson*, the

Whaleback steamship *John Ericsson* and consort barge *Alexander Holley* in one of the chambers of the Soo Locks. These two vessels were the American Steel Barge Company's share of John D. Rockefeller's famous December 1895 twelve-vessel buy for his newly organized Bessemer Steamship Company. The large letter *B* on the stacks indicates that the vessels are part of the Bessemer fleet. Source: Superior Public Museums.

ship's designers followed conventional Great Lakes practice and located the pilothouse forward atop a separate turret just behind the turret that housed the anchor handling machinery. This may well have been a requirement of the Bessemer Steamship Company specifications.

On July 25, 1898, the American Steel Barge Company launched its last whaleback ship, the 414 ft. long *Alexander McDougall*. Two years earlier *Marine Review* had speculated that once the vessels being built for the Bessemer Steamship Company were completed American Steel Barge would build another steamship to replace the tonnage sold to the Rockefeller interests, and this may have been the reason for building the *Alexander McDougall*.[22] Although equipped with a number of distinctive whaleback features such as a tapered stern, straight sheer, arched decks, and high integrity bolted hatches, this interesting ship's design incorporated a number of new features to allow her to compete with the large conventional steamships being built elsewhere on the Great Lakes. Built for its own fleet, it appears that the *Alexander McDougall* was the American Steel Barge Company's high-tech vessel that would determine if whalebacks could remain competitive in the Great Lakes ore trades. Despite his problems with Frederick Gates, the company finally honored Captain McDougall by naming a ship after him.

The *Alexander McDougall* differed from all other whaleback ships and is sometimes referred to as a semi-whaleback, as she did not feature the whaleback's signature spoon-shaped bow. Instead, this last whaleback ship was fitted with a conventional plumb bow. There were a number of reasons for combining the typical whaleback features with the conventional Great Lakes steamship plumb bow.

1. The *Alexander McDougall*'s pilothouse was placed just aft of the bow. This would have required additional buoyancy forward to prevent the ship from plunging into the sea and submerging the pilothouse. The conventional plumb bow permitted fuller hull lines and added buoyancy forward. The pilothouse was also protected by a conventional forecastle that housed the anchor handling equipment and eliminated the need for the foremost turret.
2. Great Lakes ships often used their plumb bows to advantage when maneuvering in narrow rivers. By pressing the bow against a wall they could often turn the ship in very tight quarters—a process called winding.
3. The plumb bow increased the ship's block coefficient, displacement, and the weight of cargo that could be hauled. Block coefficient is a naval architecture measure of the fullness of a ship's underwater shape.[23] Full hulls are desirable for ships hauling heavy cargos, where high speed is not required. The *Alexander McDougall*'s block coefficient at 18 ft. draft was 0.89, equal to that of the conventionally designed *Mauna Loa* launched in 1899, and higher than that for the *John Ericsson* (0.84). Providing more buoyancy forward would have reduced the bending moment flexing the hull under some load conditions. This would have reduced hull stresses and permitted design of a longer vessel.

Table 8: Block Coefficients for Later Whaleback Ships			
Hull #	Name	Cb @14 ft. wl.	Cb @18 ft. wl.
135	*John Trevor*	0.81	0.83
136	*Frank Rockefeller*	0.8	0.82
138	*John Ericsson*	0.82	0.84
141	*Alexander McDougall*	0.88	0.89
	Mauna Loa		0.89
	Conventional ship, 1899		

Alexander McDougall, the last vessel of whaleback design, sailing through the Duluth ship canal into Lake Superior. With her quadruple expansion engine, water tube boilers, and conventional bow, this state-of-the-art vessel could carry cargo loads that compared favorably with her more conventionally designed competitors. Despite this, shortly after her launch, the American Steel Barge Company announced that they would cease construction of whaleback barges and steamships. Source: UW-Superior Special Collections.

Although the *Alexander McDougall* was fitted with the same high integrity hatches as other whaleback ships, the hatches themselves were twice as wide (24 ft.) as those of the *Frank Rockefeller* (12 ft.), but still not as wide as the conventionally built *Mauna Loa* (34.5 ft.), built a year later for the Minnesota Steamship Company. To compensate for these wide hatches, the ship was fitted with two massive longitudinal girders, 24 in. deep and built from 9/16 in. plate reinforced with angles top and bottom, one on each side of the hatch beneath the main deck.[24]

The ship's machinery plant also reflected the latest developments in marine engineering practice. The *Alexander McDougall* was propelled by a quadruple expansion engine, whereas previous whaleback steamships were driven by triple expansion engines. Instead of the older Scotch marine boilers, steam was supplied by two boilers of the much newer water tube design. The *Alexander McDougall*'s power plant was, therefore, state-of-the-art and a credit to the American Steel Barge Company's young marine engineering department.[25]

A contemporary news report described *Alexander McDougall* as being magnificently fitted with electric lighting throughout, also noting that "the quarters of the officers and guests are provided with bathrooms and almost every other convenience reasonable."[26]

As the numbers in table 9 show, the *Alexander McDougall* was a well-designed ship able to haul 1,651 more tons of heavy cargo than the 16 ft. shorter conventionally designed ship *Victory* and almost as much as the 36 ft. longer *Mauna Loa*. In spite of this, following her completion, the American Steel Barge Company stopped building whaleback ships. The company would build several large barges of conventional design before being merged into the American Shipbuilding Company, formed in 1901 in the consolidation of the Great Lakes shipbuilding industry.

Table 9: Cargo Capacity in Net Tons (2,000 lb.) for Various Ships			
Name	LOA	Capacity @ 14 ft. draft	Capacity @ 18 ft. draft
John Trevor	320	2750	4100
Frank Rockefeller	380	3367	5200
John Ericsson	404	3580	6220
Alexander McDougall	414	5150	7475
Victory (Conventional ship, 1895)	398	4058	5824
Mauna Loa (Conventional ship, 1899)	450		7528

Broadly considered, whaleback ships can be grouped into three generations. The first generation was McDougall's experimental *Barge 101*. The second generation includes the thirty-five barges and steamships from *Barge 102* up to and including the steamship *John Trevor*, which was finally launched in 1895. This second generation of vessels formed the bulk of the American Steel Barge Company fleet.[27] The third generation consisted of the three steamships and two barges built after the Panic of 1893. These five unique vessels, designed by A. C. Diericx, the company's naval architect, seemingly represented intent by the company to experiment with new ideas to adapt the whaleback design to changing conditions on the Great Lakes. These five vessels were designed to work exclusively in the cargo trades of the upper Great Lakes and each exceeded the dimensions of the Welland Canal locks, putting an end to McDougall's dream of seeing his beloved whalebacks in saltwater commerce.

All five of these third-generation whaleback vessels enjoyed long lives, a testimony to the skill of their designers. The *Alexander McDougall* sailed until 1943 before being laid up and scrapped in 1946. The two barges and the *John Ericsson* hauled cargos until the mid-1960s, when these three vessels were also scrapped. The *Frank Rockefeller* was the longest sailing of the whalebacks. She hauled ore until 1927, then as the *South Park* carried a variety of cargos including sand and gravel, grain, ore, coal, and even automobiles until being converted to a tanker in 1943. Renamed *Meteor*, she hauled refined petroleum products to towns around the Great Lakes until 1969. The last surviving whaleback, she is now berthed ashore and open to visitors in Superior, Wisconsin, as the SS *Meteor* Whaleback Ship Museum.[28]

CONCLUSION

As a Great Lakes ship captain, one of Alexander McDougall's goals in inventing the whaleback ship was to produce barges and steamships that were seaworthy under the Great Lakes weather conditions that he understood. He accomplished this goal. Although seven whaleback barges and steamships were lost on the Great Lakes, the reasons had nothing to do with their design. Five of these were lost to the usual hazards of grounding or collision, and the two steamships that foundered had been significantly modified by subsequent owners.[1] Loss of the *James B. Colgate* has been attributed to leaking of the wooden hatch covers added after being sold to the Pittsburgh Steamship Company, and the *Clifton* (*Samuel Mather*), which vanished on Lake Huron in 1924, had been heavily modified with a tunnel scraper self-unloading system—an unseaworthy addition that would cause the loss of several other similarly equipped vessels of conventional design.[2]

When sent to salt water, whalebacks did not fare as well. Whaleback barges judged obsolete by their Great Lakes owners were sold to buyers on the U.S. East or Gulf Coasts, where they hauled coal or petroleum. Almost half of these foundered, often with loss of life.[3] One contemporary news account reported that "the long heavy swells along the coast played havoc with the light boats and necessitated frequent drydocking to tighten up loose rivets"; however, the blame for the loss of these vessels and crews must rest, not with the American Steel Barge Company, but with owners who chose to use them in a service for which they had not been designed.[4]

Unfortunately, designing and building seaworthy barges and steamships did not ensure their success. Owners expect successful ships to satisfy the economic requirements of their particular business. For the British ship owners who dominated international trades, this meant low operating costs, many of which were based on gross register tonnage. As discussed above, to satisfy this criteria McDougall's design had to be modified

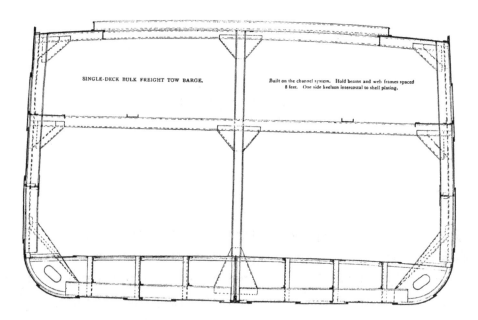

SINGLE-DECK BULK FREIGHT TOW BARGE.

Built on the channel system. Hold beams and web frames spaced
8 feet.   One side keelson intercostal to shell plating.

Midship section of a conventional steel barge C.-1882-1904 showing internal grid at beams and stanchions. Great Lakes Register 1908. Source: 1908 Great Lakes Register Rules and Regulations.

by another shipyard, resulting in the turret ship. The American Steel Barge Company's failure to interest British ship owners in the whaleback design meant that success or failure of this ship design would depend on its acceptance on the Great Lakes.

The early success of the whaleback ship on the Great Lakes apparently led John D. Rockefeller to build a few new vessels for the American Steel Barge Company and Bessemer Steamship Company fleets after the Panic of 1893. But after giving the four vessels launched in 1896 and the one launched in 1898 a short trial, the decision was made to discontinue building ships of the whaleback design. Great Lakes maritime histories offer six potential reasons for their demise.

The first reason often cited is that the whaleback's internal structure of horizontal hold beams and vertical stanchions made them difficult to unload. A corollary of this argument is that whalebacks were limited to a beam of 45 ft., as vessels wider than this required the addition of internal structure.[5]

All ships built on the Great Lakes and elsewhere during the 1890s were constructed with horizontal hold beams and vertical stanchions that were necessary to prevent hull structures from distorting when the hull flexed in a seaway; to support

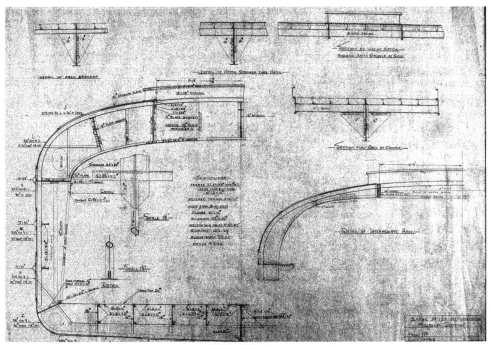

A midship section showing the changes made by Pittsburgh Steamship Company to the whaleback steamship *John B. Trevor* to eliminate internal structures that interfered with mechanized unloading equipment. The left side of the drawing shows the widely spaced arches added, and the right side shows the structure between the arches. McDougall's flush steel plate hatches have been replaced by much easier to handle wooden hatch covers set into raised steel coamings. Source: Bowling Green State University Special Collections.

side framing from water pressure and localized loads; and to limit the unsupported span of deck beams. Whaleback ships were therefore no different from any other ships in this regard. Naval architects were able to dispense with this interfering internal structure in the construction of the *Agustus B. Wolvin* in 1904 by reinforcing her hull with a series of large arches.[6] The Pittsburgh Steamship Company, which owned the whaleback ships of the American Steel Barge Company and Bessemer fleets by 1904, responded by fitting large arches to its larger whaleback steamships and barges and removing the internal stanchions and hold beams to provide unrestricted cargo holds.[7] This argument can therefore be dismissed.

Likewise, the argument that internal structure limited the beam of whaleback ships to 45 ft. is spurious. An examination of whaleback ship drawings shows that the 50 ft. wide *Alexander McDougall* was constructed with the same internal structural support as the 36 ft. wide *Colgate Hoyt*.

The second reason is that the whalebacks' small hatches made them difficult and costly to unload. This argument has been made by both Alexander McDougall and his later business associate Julius Barnes.[8] As unloading equipment became increasingly mechanized during the 1890s, there is no question that the small hatches on whaleback ships made it hard to unload bulk cargos such as iron ore and coal. Whether this increased the whaleback's cost of operation, at least prior to 1893, is a different matter. Industry custom was to charge unloading of iron ore to the vessel at the fixed rate of nineteen and a half cents per ton. American Steel Barge Company records for 1891 indicate that whaleback ships paid this rate, as did operators of conventional vessels.[9] Although the whalebacks with their narrow hatches could be unloaded for the same cost as their competitors' ships of conventional design, unloading difficulties would have slowed port turnaround, or "dispatch." This would have resulted in fewer trips, less cargo, and less revenue.

With the design of the *Alexander McDougall*, built with 24 ft. wide hatches (twice the width of previous whaleback ships), the American Steel Barge Company's engineering department attempted to correct this problem. In spite of this, the company decided to cease production of whaleback ships before the *Alexander McDougall* could be given a thorough trial.

A related problem not mentioned by McDougall concerned the design of the hatch closures. An integral feature of McDougall's invention was the use of high integrity steel plate bolted hatch closures. McDougall evidently felt that the usual wooden hatch covers protected with tarpaulins would not stand up to the rigors of wind and water on the whalebacks' unprotected decks.

McDougall seems to have been oblivious to the limits of human endurance, whether building *Barge 101* on an unimproved shoreline, handling material in his shipyard without mechanized equipment, expecting crews to sail halfway around the world while living under conditions condemned by British shipping authorities as inadequate, or moving about the curved decks of a whaleback in a seaway. Robert Clark sums up McDougall's attitude as "Nothing to it, only the nerve to tackle the job," and McDougall's design of his ships' hatch covers appears to be in line with this philosophy.[10] Each of the 3/8 in. thick, 12 ft. by 8 ft. steel hatch covers on the whaleback steamship *Frank Rockefeller* would have weighed 1,470 lbs., and each cover would have been secured by close to 100 stud bolts screwed into the deck plating and dogged down tight. In his memoir, Captain Merwin Stone Thompson, who sailed on the whaleback steamship *John Ericsson*, describes the backbreaking labor involved.

> Here was the real catch; her new heavy steel plate type hatches, almost impossible to handle, had to be secured with stud bolts, hundreds of them. All of this was in place of the old style wooden sectional hatches which could be handled by four men. Remember, I am quoting the year 1896. This operation in many instances delayed the ship after loading and required most of the forward crew on and off watch to complete the job. In most cases when the weather would permit, we would leave port with the hatches partially secured, all men working overtime sometimes one or two hours while in-route. The same situation was reversed when approaching our unloading port.
>
> The stud bolts were stored at each end of the ship. Shortly after leaving port on one trip, I was off watch working on these bolts at the end of the number three hatch, when a deckhand appeared with two small buckets of bolts, one in each hand. When about opposite me with the ship rolling slightly, he slipped and fell. One of the buckets went overboard and he was on his way when I fortunately could pull him back from the rounding top side of the ship.
>
> This news spread like wildfire around the lakes and it was soon getting easy to get a job on the *Ericsson*. That was the reason for her nick-name, the floating workhouse.[11]

While ship owners of the time may have considered crews to be replaceable, time lost was not, and the time required to remove or replace these cumbersome hatch covers four times each trip would certainly have contributed to the vessels' slow dispatch, to say nothing of the additional problems that these crews would face when the plating surrounding the hatch openings had been bent or dinged by the swinging clam shell buckets of the Brown hoists used to unload ore in the 1890s.

About 1910, in conjunction with the structural modifications described above, the Pittsburgh Steamship Company enlarged the hatches of the larger whalebacks in their fleet and replaced McDougall's steel plate hatches with standard wooden sectional covers set in raised coamings.[12] In doing so the company apparently was willing to gamble that it could operate its ships safely without the bolted high integrity hatches. It was largely able to do so, although failure of these wooden hatch covers was responsible for the foundering with heavy loss of life of the whaleback steamship *James B. Colgate* on Lake Erie in 1916, one year after being sold by Pittsburgh Steamship to new owners.[13]

Alexander McDougall's high integrity hatch design was actually similar to the steel plate hatch covers now used on Great Lakes ships, but these covers are handled with traveling electric gantry cranes, and the hundreds of bolts have been replaced with quick-acting lever-actuated clamps. McDougall's hatch covers were ahead of their time; his idea was sound, but the technology had not been developed in the 1890s to make them practical.[14]

The third potential reason given for the demise of the whaleback is that the underwater shape of the hull resulted in less displacement, limiting its ability to float heavy cargo. According to Professor Harry Benford, a naval architect and marine transportation economics expert,

> McDougall's first designs were for escort (towed) barges, where the cutaway forefoot would have reduced the tendency to yaw. In powered vessels it would also lend itself to excellent ice-breaking capabilities. On the other hand, it would lessen the waterline length, so reducing displacement and cargo capacity, while increasing wave-making resistance. Elementary economic analysis shows that the most profitable Great Lakes bulk carrier is one whose length and beam approximate the internal dimensions of the Poe Lock and whose hull form comes dismayingly close to doing the same. Clearly, the whaleback fails to meet that last specification.[15]

Anyone looking at the hull of a modern Great Lakes 1,000 ft. ore carrier will appreciate the accuracy of Professor Benford's comment, but in the 1890s, this was in the future. While the whaleback hull form caused the ships to displace less than their conventionally built counterparts, their light hull structure allowed more of their displacement to be used to haul cargo. Table 9 shows that their actual cargo hauling capacity was high compared to that of their contemporaries. For example, on an 18 ft. waterline *John Ericsson* could haul 6,220 tons of a heavy cargo, compared to 5,824 tons for the similar-sized, conventionally built *Victory*.

The fourth problem is that the whaleback ships were more expensive than ships of a conventional design. One author claimed that by 1898 whaleback ships simply cost more than their conventional counterparts.[16]

Between 1896 and 1899 the company built four large barges: the whalebacks *Barge 137* and *Alexander Holley* and the conventionally designed *Constitution* and *Maida*. Table 10 provides cost data for these four vessels. These figures show that by the late 1890s it did cost more for the American Steel Barge Company to build a whaleback barge than a conventional one. The differences in labor costs are particularly significant. Since the idea behind the whaleback ship was to produce low freeboard vessels that could haul more cargo for their hull size, using gross tonnage as the denominator for this comparison is not entirely appropriate, but the differences are striking enough to conclude that by the late 1890s it was difficult to build large whaleback vessels with their necessary structural reinforcement as inexpensively as conventional ones.

Table 10: Costs Comparison for Late American Steel Barge Company Barges					
Hull #	Vessel Name	Gross Tonnage	Cost Per Gross Ton	Labor Cost Per Gross Ton	Vessel Type
137	*Barge 137*	2,841	46.72	16.12	Whaleback
139	*Alexander Holley*	2,721	48.01	20.11	Whaleback
140	*Constitution*	3,231	35.43	13	Conventional
142	*Maida*	3,474	32.19	11.62	Conventional
Sources: McDougall, "Account Book"; Great Lakes Vessel Database.					

The fifth problem with the whaleback ships is that they were too small. McDougall developed his idea for whaleback ships in 1880, when the practice on the Great Lakes for shipping bulk cargos involved several consort barges pulled by a freight-carrying, steam-powered towboat. Unfortunately, it took so long for him to obtain financing and to organize a business that he only had about four years to gain acceptance for his concept before shipbuilding activities were halted by the Panic of 1893. When business resumed in 1896, ship owners on the Great Lakes realized that one large ship was much more economical than a small steamship towing one or more small barges. While consort barges continued to be built in the late 1890s, the trend for ship owners was to specify larger and larger vessels.[17] By 1896, ship owners were requesting 400 ft. ships, and by 1898, when the 414 ft. *Alexander McDougall* was built, other shipbuilders were producing ships up to 450 ft. long. By 1900, shipbuilders were producing 500 ft. ships, and by 1906, 600-footers.[18] Designers of whaleback ships were at a particular disadvantage in this respect. The whaleback hull form is what structural engineers would consider to be a structurally inefficient hull shape compared to conventional ships with their rectangular cross sections. It is therefore entirely possible that by 1898 the American Steel Barge Company realized that it could not win this size race and decided to stop producing whaleback ships.

The sixth major reason for the demise of the whaleback is that the ships were not suited to the changing business environment. Prior to 1896, the American Steel Barge Company was an independent organization dedicated to building and operating ships of the whaleback design; its own fleet operated almost all of the barges and steamships that it built. Charters to haul bulk cargos were obtained on the commodity market; shippers contracted with ship operators to deliver cargos at a fixed rate without regard to the type of ship used. Costs for unloading cargos were charged to the vessel or to the shipper at fixed rates established by industry custom. Since the same shipping rates and unloading costs applied equally to all shippers, and since the American Steel Barge Company operated only its own ships, competition with conventionally designed vessels was indirect.

All of this changed with the consolidation of the iron mining industry and with the formation of dedicated fleets controlled by the mine owners. Fleets like the Bessemer Steamship Company became part of an integrated transportation system; they were dedicated to moving ore from mine to mill at the lowest possible cost.[19] As these iron mining companies became vertically integrated, they also gained control of the loading and unloading docks, so costs associated with these activities also came under scrutiny. There was an incentive for these new integrated ore producers to carefully control all costs, and the ships in their fleets were no exception.[20] Small ships and ships that were hard to unload were weeded out of their fleets, and new ones built to these old designs were not purchased. In 1896 Pickands Mather bought 400 ft. ships for the new Bessemer Fleet. Ten years later, Pittsburgh Steamship Company, the Bessemer Fleet's successor, was buying 600 ft. ships.

It would therefore appear that McDougall's whalebacks were successful when the Great Lakes bulk shipping paradigm was based on strings of small towed barges able to easily navigate small lock chambers and narrow, shallow channels, even though some intended advantages were sacrificed to produce practical vessels. Once locks were enlarged, harbors and channels improved, and the structural design of ship hulls was better understood, ship owners abandoned the towed consort system in favor of single very large steamships. The American Steel Barge's inability to build the easy to unload, increasingly longer whaleback ships demanded by the new integrated iron ore producers at a competitive price ultimately doomed the whaleback ship.

Epilogue

The saga of the whaleback ships and the men who imagined them and built them did not end with the 1898 launch of the whaleback steamship *Alexander McDougall*. The ships still had economic value although, for some, not in the trades for which they had been designed. The men who built them still had years of productive work ahead of them, and McDougall would continue with his remarkable career.

Alexander McDougall

On May 16, 1899, seven Great Lakes shipbuilders merged to form the American Ship Building Company.[1] Included in this consolidation was the American Steel Barge Company. On May 18, *Marine Review* reported, "Friday last Alexander McDougall turned over to the American Shipbuilding Company, the affairs of the American Steel Barge Company at West Superior."[2]

McDougall was fifty-four years old; he had stayed until the end, although with diminished influence and responsibility following the events of 1893. In his autobiography he wrote, "By the end of the year [1893] I was stripped of nearly everything that I had."[3] Still, by the beginning of 1899 he had enough money to start two new businesses: a steamship agency in partnership with A. D. Thompson and a new shipyard at Collingwood, Ontario. He continued with projects in western mining, Mississippi River shipping, and the cold storage business. He was one of the founders as well as the first president of the Highland Canal & Power Company, the forerunner of the current Minnesota Power.[4]

In 1915 McDougall again entered the shipbuilding business in the Duluth–Superior area to build a new rectangular ship of his design that could reach salt water from the lakes via the New York State canal system. America's 1917 entry into World War I interfered with his plans after he had built one vessel at his old shipyard in Duluth where he had built *Barge 101*. With his partner Julius Barnes he then moved up the St. Louis River, bought a large tract of land, and established a shipyard and planned community named Riverside. This huge project was completed quickly. Between the time the shipyard opened in 1917 and its closure in 1921, it built forty-four ships: thirty-nine 250 ft. Fredrikstad ocean-going cargo ships, and five motor vessels able to transit the New York State Barge Canal. One of these, the *Day Peckinpaugh*, originally built as the *I.L.I. 101*, is maintained today by the State of New York as a museum.[5]

As a measure of his astonishing energy and enterprise, McDougall was awarded thirty-four American patents between the years 1900 and 1923.[6] Captain Alexander McDougall died on May 22, 1923, at the age of seventy-eight, at his home, which still stands at 2201 East Second Street, Duluth, Minnesota.[7]

The Shipbuilders

Robert Clark left the American Steel Barge Company in the fall of 1892, supposedly to start his own barge company in West Duluth. According to historian Richard Wright this effort was unsuccessful.[8] In November 1896 Alexander McDougall wrote a letter of recommendation for him as he was apparently looking for a job.[9] He moved to the San Francisco Bay area around 1898 and finished his career there working for the U.S. government.[10] Joseph Kidd, promoted to manage the shipyard in spite of Charles Wetmore's misgivings, left the American Steel Barge Company in 1897, and on April 29 *Marine Review* reported that he was "about to undertake consulting engineering work at Duluth."[11] Ten months later, known as Captain Joseph Kidd, he was commenting on the practicality of salvaging the sunken battleship USS *Maine* in Havana Harbor. In the fall of 1899 the *Marine Record* reported that he was considered to be the best marine surveyor at the head of the lakes.[12] A marine directory published in 1903 listed him under *Designers of all Classes of Vessels* with offices at 610 Board of Trade, Duluth.[13] In his book *Pigs at Sea*, author David Frew places Kidd at Alexander McDougall's side constructing Fredrikstad ships during World War I, but no evidence has been found to support this claim.[14]

The house at 2201 East Second Street in Duluth, Minnesota, which Alexander McDougall built around 1912, was to be his last home. In his autobiography, McDougall says that he installed a workshop and water tanks in the basement where he could build and experiment with ship models. The current owners of this meticulously maintained residence say that no trace of these exist today. Source: Superior Public Museums.

Hugh Calderwood, dispatched by the American Steel Barge Company to manage Pacific Steel Barge Company, returned to Wisconsin and was chief draftsman and superintendent of the West Superior yard when he was hired by McDougall in 1900 to run the new shipyard at Collingwood, Ontario.[15] While at Collingwood, Calderwood was credited with the design of a number of ships including the SS *Huronic*, a successful large, high-class passenger steamer built for the Northern Navigation Company in 1902. *Marine Review* reported that Calderwood's design was approved by noted Great Lakes naval architect Frank Kirby.[16] The marine press continued to report Calderwood's activities at Collingwood, and as the years went by he seemed to be more responsible for designing and supervising construction of ships than actually running the yard.

A. C. Diericx remained with the American Steel Barge Company until it merged into the American Shipbuilding Company, and the marine press reported that his wife christened several of the ships that he designed. He was transferred by the newly merged company to their Cleveland, Ohio, headquarters to become head of the hull drafting department.[17]

When the decision was made in late 1894 to hire Pickands Mather to manage the American Steel Barge Company fleet, Angus McDougall, manager of the company's operating department, was out of a job. On January 24, 1895, *Marine Review* announced that Angus McDougall would open an insurance and brokerage business in Duluth.[18] Ten years later this Captain McDougall was surveying the steamship *Minnie M.* after she lost her propeller, so perhaps by this time he was working for insurers to resolve marine casualty claims.[19]

Nothing is known of the subsequent careers of William Mahon or Frank Hayes, designers of the whaleback ships' machinery, or of Joseph Crawford, who would have been responsible for keeping materials flowing to a shipyard on the edge of the frontier. This is unfortunate; judging from their work, they must have been talented, capable, and hard-working individuals.

The Whaleback Ships

In 1900 the American Steel Barge Company's fleet consisted of nineteen whaleback barges and ten steamships. *Barge 101* had been sold in 1899, and *Barges 104* and *115* had been lost in 1898 and 1899—both washed ashore after losing their tow lines. *Barges 102* and *103* had been previously sold to the Bessemer Steamship Company.[20] The remaining twenty-nine vessels were merged into John D. Rockefeller's Bessemer Steamship Company fleet in 1900, and then in 1901 into the Pittsburgh Steamship subsidiary of the newly formed U.S. Steel Corporation. The whaleback steamship *Thomas Wilson* was sunk in 1902 off the Duluth harbor after being damaged in a collision with another vessel. She lies there still, one mile from the harbor's north pier, a popular local dive attraction and target of electronic fish finders on charter fishing boats.[21]

In 1905, Pittsburgh Steamship began to dispose of smaller inefficient vessels, and a number of small whaleback steamships and barges were sent to the East Coast.[22] Placed in the coastal coal trade, they came full circle, again competing with wooden schooners as they had been intended to do on the lakes fifteen years earlier.[23] Several of these barges were sold to owners on the U.S. Gulf Coast and converted to tank barges.[24] In the coastal trades, these vessels, in addition to serving in an environment for which they were not designed, were subject to the usual inshore navigation hazards of grounding and collision. Few survived long enough to be cut up for scrap.

In the early 1900s Pittsburgh Steamship began a program to modernize its remaining vessels. Horizontal mooring winches to handle wire rope mooring lines were added in 1905, and around 1910 the changes to hull structure and hatches were made. These changes allowed the larger whalebacks to work as productive units of the Pittsburgh fleet into 1924.[25] By the late 1920s all of the barges and all of the steamships except the *Alexander McDougall* had been sold, the larger vessels to organizations around the lakes where they often worked in the sand and gravel trades. The Nicholson organization of Detroit used at least two whalebacks to haul new cars to distribution points along the lakes. *Alexander McDougall*, the last whaleback in the Pittsburgh Steamship fleet, was finally sold to the Buckeye Steamship Company in 1936.[26]

At the outset of World War II, five whalebacks were left on the lakes: the *South Park* (*Frank Rockefeller*), the *John Ericsson*, the *Alexander McDougall*, the barge *Alexander Holley*, and *Barge 137*. There is no question that the war extended their lives. The *Alexander McDougall* was scrapped shortly after the war, but the four other whalebacks continued to sail into the mid-1950s.[27]

The last whaleback sailing the lakes was the venerable *Frank Rockefeller*, under her third name, *Meteor*. Hauling refined petroleum products for Cleveland Tankers, she continued to sail until 1969, when she damaged her bottom plating on a rocky shoal off Lake Superior's Keweenaw Peninsula.[28] In the ensuing investigation, the Coast Guard refused to allow the aging single-hulled tanker to continue to sail. She was eventually donated to a historical preservation group in Superior, Wisconsin, and remains open seasonally for public tours.

Frank Rockefeller sailing as a unit of the Pittsburgh Steamship Company c. 1916. A number of changes made by the company are evident. Steam deck winches have been added to handle wire rope mooring lines, steel plate hatch covers have been replaced with wooden hatch covers set in raised steel coamings, and a large coal bunker has been erected on the deck forward of the after turret. The smokestack has been painted in the Pittsburgh Steamship colors—a silver stack with black smoke band around the top. Source: Superior Public Museums.

The American Steel Barge Company West Superior Shipyard

Replacing Joe Kidd as a shipyard superintendent after 1897 was Daniel E. Ford, who had supervised construction of ships for Rockefeller.[29] Managing the yard during a period of decreased activity, Ford's principal accomplishment was its modernization. Improvements included pneumatic riveting, electrification of machinery that had previously been operated by steam, a huge gantry crane over the building ways, and a new machine shop.[30] It appears that the Rockefeller-controlled syndicate that owned the yard intended to continue to build ships other than whalebacks. But, as with the Panic of 1893, the yard was overtaken by outside events sweeping the country, this time a consolidation of the Great Lakes shipbuilding industry.

After being merged into the newly formed American Shipbuilding Company, the West Superior shipyard continued to build ships. Prior to World War I the yard built conventional Great Lakes barges and steamships including the *Edward Y. Townsend*, which at the time of her launch in 1906 was the largest steamship (by measured tonnage) on the Great Lakes.[31] During the Great War the yard built Fredrikstad ships of the same design as those being built at the McDougall Duluth Riverside yard.

In 1919 American Shipbuilding decided to stop building at its West Superior yard, but the yard remained open because of its remote location at the western tip of Lake Superior. Ship owners realized the advantages of a drydock and shipyard available to repair ships damaged on the lake. During World War II, the yard was largely inactive and did not participate in the wartime shipbuilding boom taking place elsewhere around the Duluth–Superior waterfront.[32]

In 1945 the yard was sold, and it passed through several different owners over the years. From the mid-1950s through the early 1980s the yard completed a number of large modernization projects: bow thruster installations, self-unloader conversions, and hull lengthenings. In 1990 the yard completed a major project by shortening a vessel—a 120 ft. section was removed from the *Leon Fraser* to produce the 520 ft. bulk cement carrier *Alpena*.[33]

Now named Fraser Shipyards, Inc., the company operates a sixty-acre building and repair yard with machine and fabricating facilities, water berths, and two drydocks. Each year, vessels of the American lakes fleet brave the ice in the Duluth–Superior harbor to arrive for their winter layup. Their arrival date depends on the state of the economy as they try to squeeze one last cargo into their schedule. Ships are moored at the yard, docked in one of the drydocks, or tied up at docks along the harbor while Fraser's shipwrights, boiler makers, mechanics, electricians, and other trades tend to their winter maintenance needs.

Appendix A

Whaleback Vessel Dimension Conventions

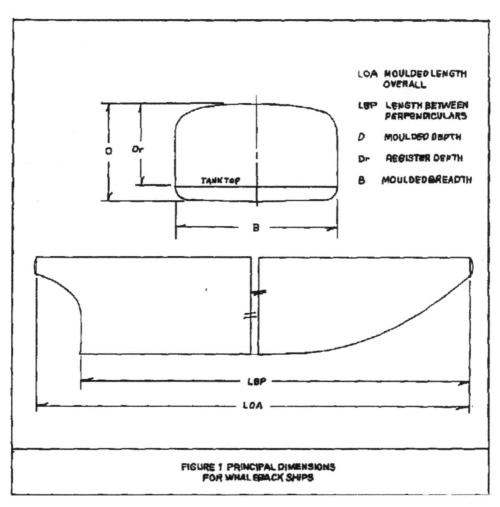

LOA MOULDED LENGTH OVERALL

LBP LENGTH BETWEEN PERPENDICULARS

D MOULDED DEPTH

Dr REGISTER DEPTH

B MOULDED BREADTH

TANK TOP

B

LBP

LOA

FIGURE 1 PRINCIPAL DIMENSIONS FOR WHALEBACK SHIPS

Source: Author's drawing.

Appendix B

A Brief Explanation of Relevant Shipping Terminology

Linear Measurements

Beam. The width of the vessel's hull measured at its widest part. When measured for the purpose of calculating register tonnage it does not include the thickness of the vessel's shell plating.

Depth. Measured vertically from the main deck (called the spar deck in Great Lakes ships) to the ship's bottom.

Register Depth. As above, except the thickness of the deck plating and the height of the doublebottom is deducted. This is the depth often published in shipping registers.

Draft. The amount of water required to float the ship. For merchant vessels, this subject can be confusing as people familiar with recreational watercraft tend to think of draft as a fixed number. For merchant vessels, especially those trading on the Great Lakes in the whaleback era, draft varies depending on the cargo carried, the way it is stowed and the lake level that influenced the water depth in the shipping channel.

Trim. The difference in draft between the ship's bow and stern.

Length overall (LOA). The length of the vessel from the front of the bow to the tip of the stern. This is the length dimension used by the American Steel Barge Company to describe their vessels.

Register Length. The length dimension used by authorities when calculating tonnage. This is the length dimension usually published in various shipping registers. For whaleback vessels it does not include the length of the hull aft of the sternpost. Therefore the length of the whaleback steamship *Meteor* (ex. *Frank Rockefeller*) could be either 380 ft. or 367 ft. Both are correct.

Weight Measurements

Displacement (Displ). The overall weight of a ship, which according to the Greek philosopher Archimedes is equal to the vessel's underwater volume multiplied by the density of the water in which it floats. Displacement depends on the ship's loading. For example, light ship displacement is the displacement of the ship without cargo, fuel, and consumable stores. As cargo is loaded, displacement increases in an amount equal to the weight of the added cargo.

Cargo at a Specified Waterline (Cargo @ XX WL). Waterlines are horizontal lines drawn on a vessel's hull lines drawing. They are usually drawn parallel to the vessel's keel. For example, a 14 ft. waterline would represent a line 14 ft. above a vessel's keel. By calculating the displacement of the ship at a known waterline and knowing the weight of the vessel's light displacement and the weight of fuel and other consumables, the naval architect can predict the weight of cargo that can be carried with the ship floating at this waterline.

Long Ton (2,240 1bs.). In medieval times, the weight of a standard barrel of wine was called a *tun*. For most of the twentieth century, this was the measure of weight used in the shipping industry throughout the English-speaking world. Iron ore shipped on the Great Lakes is measured in long tons.

Short Ton (2,000 1bs.). The definition of the measure of weight used in commerce in the United States. On the Great Lakes, coal was measured in short tons. Sometimes referred to as Net or Nett tons by Alexander McDougall in his writings.

Block Coefficient (Cb). Not a measure of weight, but related to displacement. Block coefficient measures the ratio of the underwater volume of a ship's hull to that of a rectangular block with dimensions equal to the ship's length, beam, and draft. A block coefficient for a modern Great Lakes 1,000 footer could be over 0.9, that for a Navy destroyer about 0.5.

Tonnage Measurements

Tonnage is a confusing subject that despite its name is a measure of volume, not weight. In medieval times, wine was shipped in barrels called tuns. In England the king wished to tax arriving ships based on their earning potential. Other authorities also wished to levy fees on the same basis. The most convenient measure was to determine for each vessel, the number of tuns that she could carry. This idea is still used today but the system for calculating tonnage has evolved into a complex set of rules. One "ton" is considered to be 100 cubic feet. The term **"Register Tonnage"** refers to this concept of measuring volume, not weight.

Gross Tonnage (G.T.). An attempt to measure the enclosed internal volume of a ship. An entry in a shipping news about the "10,000 Ton, or more specifically the 10,000 Gross Ton "Rust Bucket" is referring to this gross tonnage (volume) not its displacement (weight).

Net Tonnage. An attempt to measure the ship's actual cargo carrying volume. In the whaleback era, this was done through a complex set of rules that excluded some spaces and provided deductions to account for others. These deductions were then subtracted from the vessel's gross tonnage to arrive at its net tonnage.

It was, of course, the naval architect's job to minimize gross and net tonnage without jeopardizing actual cargo-carrying capacity or seaworthiness. This has resulted over the years in a number of "rulebeaters," a prime example being the Doxford turret ship.

Unfortunately, Alexander McDougall himself is not always clear in his correspondence when he writes "tons" whether he means volume or weight. For example, when he refers to *Barge 102* as a vessel of 1,500 ton capacity he is almost certainly referring to its tonnage. However, in his account book, the entry referring to capacity for the same vessel appears to mean cargo weight. I have to the best of my ability tried to not confuse the two ideas.

APPENDIX C

Whaleback Barges and Steamships with Principal Dimensions

Hull #	Year Launched	LOA	Beam	Depth	Name	Description
101	1888	137	25	19		Original Whaleback Barge
36 ft. × 22 ft. Ships						
102	1889	260	36	22		Improved Barge Design—Prototype for All Subsequent Whaleback Ships
103	1890	260	36	22		
104	1890	284	36	22		A Series of Barges—A Lengthened 102
105	1890	284	36	22		
107	1890	284	36	22		
117	1891	284	36	22		
118	1891	284	36	22		
106	1890	284	36	22	*Colegate Hoyt*	First Whaleback Steamship
109	1890	264	36	22		Series of "Canal Sized" Shortened 104
110	1891	264	36	22		
111	1891	264	36	22		
115	1891	264	36	22		
116	1891	264	36	22		
126	1892	264	36	22		
127	1892	264	36	22		
108	1891	264	36	22	*Joseph L. Colby*	Canal Sized Steamship

Hull #	Year Launched	LOA	Beam	Depth	Name	Description
129	1893	292	36	22		Series of 292 ft. Barges—Lengthened 104
130	1893	292	36	22		
131	1893	292	36	22		
132	1893	292	36	22		
133	1893	292	36	22		
134	1893	292	36	22		
38 ft. × 24 ft. Ships						
112	1891	264	38	24	*C. W. Wetmore*	Canal Sized Steamships
113	1891	264	38	24	*E. B. Bartlett*	*Wetmore* Sailed on Salt Water
114	1891	264	38	24	*A. D. Thompson*	
119	1892	320	38	24	*Thomas Wilson*	
120	1892	320	38	24	*Samuel Mather*	
121	1892	320	38	24	*James B. Colgate*	
135	1895	320	38	24	*J. B. Trevor*	
122	1892	320	38	24	*Sagamore*	Barge Version of 119–121
42 ft. × 25.5 ft. Ships						
123	1892	340	42	26	*Pathfinder*	
124	1892	320	42	26	*Washburn*	Two Package
125	1892	320	42	26	*Pillsbury*	Freighters
45 ft. × 26 ft. Ships						
136	1896	380	45	26	*Frank Rockefeller*	Still Exists as *Meteor*
137	1896	380	45	26		Barge Version of 136
32ft. × 20 ft. Ships						
201	1890	190	32	20		Two Whaleback Barges Built on the East Coast Later Lengthened
202	1890	190	32	20		

Hull #	Year Launched	LOA	Beam	Depth	Name	Description
Unique Designs						
138	1896	404	48	27	*John Ericcson*	Last True Whaleback Steamship
139	1896	376	48	26	*Alexander Holly*	Barge Consort for *John Ericcson*
141	1898	414	50	27	*Alexander McDougall*	Built with a Whaleback Stern and Hull But Conventional Bow
128	1893	360	42	24	*Christopher Columbus*	Passenger Vessel
145	1894	360	42	27	*City of Everett*	Whaleback Steamship Built Everett, WA
	1893	320	38	25	*Sagamore*	Whaleback Steamship Built in England License

NOTES

CHAPTER 1

1. McDougall, *Autobiography of Captain Alexander McDougall*, 3.
2. Ibid., 9.
3. Meakin, *Master of the Inland Seas*, 8.
4. McDougall, *Autobiography of Captain Alexander McDougall*, 12–13.
5. Ibid., 14–16.
6. Ibid., 20.
7. Ibid., 30.
8. Ibid., 32.
9. Thomas, *British Ocean Tramps*, I: 24.
10. Workman, *Shipping on the Great Lakes*, 364.
11. Bowlus, *Iron Ore Transport on the Great Lakes*, 100, 134, 164.
12. Ibid., 65–69.
13. Paris, *The Sesquicentennial History of the St. Marys Falls Canal*.
14. *Brief History of the Welland Canal*, available at www.wellandcanal.com.
15. Gilmore, *The St. Lawrence River Canal Vessel*.
16. Paris, *The Sesquicentennial History of the St. Marys Falls Canal*.
17. Bowlus, *Iron Ore Transport on the Great Lakes*, 95–99.
18. Ibid., 114–15, 151.
19. Hilton, *Lake Michigan Passenger Steamers*, 84–87.
20. Lenihan, *Shipwrecks of Isle Royal National Park*, 34.
21. Ibid., 35; Clark, *Genesis of the Whaleback Ship*, n.p.
22. Corlett, *The Iron Ship*, 8.
23. Lenihan, *Shipwrecks of Isle Royal National Park*, 35; Rodgers, *Guardian of the Lakes*, chap. 1.
24. McCarthy, *Ships Fastenings*, chap 12; Arnott, *Design and Construction of Steel Merchant Ships*, chap. 5, section I; Abell, *The Shipwrights' Trade*, 139.
25. *Riveted Joint Efficiency*—Personal communication between Garzke and author.

26. Garzke and Woodward, *Titanic Ships, Titanic Disasters*, 27–29.

27. Arnott, *Design and Construction of Steel Merchant Ships*, 83–89.

28. Quoted in Arnott, *Design and Construction of Steel Merchant Ships*, 86.

29. Pellett, *The Machinery of the Steamship* Meteor.

30. Benford, *Naval Architecture of Non-Naval Architects*, 138; Arnott, *Design and Construction of Steel Merchant Ships*, 66.

31. Meakin, *Master of the Inland Sea*, 20; Snow and Lee, *A Shipyard in Maine*, 20–21.

32. Chernow, *Titan*.

33. Rossell and Chapman, *Principles of Naval Architecture*, chap. 2.

34. *Marine Review*, bound copies, 1893.

CHAPTER 2

1. McDougall, *Autobiography of Captain Alexander McDougall*, 32.

2. McDougall, U.S. Patent 241,813, March 9, 1880.

3. McDougall, U.S. Patent 259,889, April 4, 1882.

4. McDougall, U.S. Patent 393,997, April 18, 1888.

5. Ibid.

6. Clark, "The Advent of the Whalebacks on the Great Lakes," *Nor'easter* 23, no. 5 (September–October).

7. *Great Lakes Vessels Online Index*, Historical Collections of the Great Lakes, Bowling Green State University, available at www.bgsu.edu/cgi-bin/xvs12.cgi, *Barge 101*.

8. Author's personal experience.

9. Thiesen, *Industrializing American Shipbuilding*, 54–58.

10. Chapelle, *The Search for Speed under Sail*, 413.

11. Herreshoff, *Captain Nat Herreshoff*, 129; Attwood and Cooper, *A Textbook of Laying Off*.

12. Clark, "The Advent of the Whalebacks on the Great Lakes," *Nor'easter* 23, no. 5 (September–October).

13. Entries 957 and 958, Roll 33, American Steel Barge Company, Naval Architectural Drawings, American Shipbuilding Co. and Predecessors, Historical Collection of the Great Lakes, Bowling Green State University.

14. Clark, "The Advent of the Whalebacks on the Great Lakes," *Nor'easter* 23, no. 5 (September–October).

15. Babcock, "System of Work in a Great Lakes Shipyard"; Curr, *Lake Shipyard Methods of Steel Ship Construction*, 1907.

16. Throughout this book length of barges and steamships is "length overall," which is the dimension used by the American Steel Barge Company. Other documents such as legal descriptions use "length between perpendiculars," which for whalebacks excludes the length from the sternpost to the stern. *Great Lakes Vessels Online Index*: Gross

Register Tonnage is a legal description of the internal volume of a vessel. It is based on a ton of cargo requiring a volume of 100 cu. ft. Actual cargo capacity will therefore depend on what is carried. McDougall says that *Barge 101* carried 1,200 tons of iron ore on her first voyage. The 1,500 tons burden mentioned in the *Chicago Tribune* quote probably relates to her maximum capacity hauling iron ore.

17. Entries 957 and 958, Roll 33, American Steel Barge Company, Naval Architectural Drawings, American Shipbuilding Co. and Predecessors, Historical Collection of the Great Lakes, Bowling Green State University.
18. Benford, *Naval Architecture for Non-Naval Architects*, 84; Benford, *Great Storm of 1913*, May 13, 2005.
19. Holms, *Practical Shipbuilding*, 83, 67.
20. Thomas, *British Ocean Tramps*, I: 24.
21. Thompson, *An Ancient Mariner Reflects*, 46.
22. McDougall, *Autobiography of Captain Alexander McDougall*, 32.
23. For example, see Wright, *Freshwater Whales*, 43. A vessel with a cylindrical or nearly cylindrical cross section would have less internal volume to haul cargo and would not have possessed sufficient transverse stability to be seaworthy.
24. *Chicago Tribune*, quoted in McDougall, *Autobiography of Captain Alexander McDougall*.
25. Clark, "The Advent of the Whalebacks on the Great Lakes," *Nor'easter* 23, no. 5 (September–October).
26. Ibid.
27. Ibid.
28. Joseph Colby to Wetmore, November 28, 1888.
29. King, *The Mesabi Road*, 24; Bowlus, *Iron Ore Transport on the Great Lakes*, 58, 138.
30. Bowlus, *Iron Ore Transport on the Great Lakes*, 123–30.
31. Thompson, *Queen of the Lakes*, 333.

CHAPTER 3

1. Beck, "The History and Significance of the S.S. *Meteor*," 5.
2. Meakin, *Master of the Inland Sea*, 32.
3. www.scottwinslow.com/manufacturer/HOYT/COLGATE/2900.
4. Charles Colby to C. W. Wetmore, November 28, 1888.
5. McDougall, Hoyt, and Wetmore, Memorandum of Agreement, December 22, 1888.
6. Charles Colby to C. W. Wetmore, December 4, 1888; *Great Lakes Vessels Online Index*, Historical Collections of the Great Lakes, Bowling Green State University, available at www.bgsu.edu/cgi-bin/xvs12.cgi.
7. Clark, "The Advent of the Whalebacks on the Great Lakes," *Nor'easter* 23, no. 5 (September–October).
8. McDougall, *Autobiography of Captain Alexander McDougall*, 49.
9. Alexander McDougall to Colgate Hoyt, August 14, 1889.

10. Clark, "The Advent of the Whalebacks on the Great Lakes," *Nor'easter* 23, no. 5 (September–October); Ida Strong to Ken Thro, May 1, 1987, Superior Public Museums Collection.

11. McDougall, *Autobiography of Captain Alexander McDougall*, 34; Wright, *Freshwater Whales*, 44.

12. C. W. Wetmore to Colgate Hoyt, 1892.

13. Daley, *Duluth's Other Company Town*, 33.

14. Gates, *The Chapters of My Life*, xx; Chernow, *Titan*, 367–68.

15. Meakin, *Master of the Inland Seas*, 32.

16. Alexander McDougall to C. W. Wetmore, May 5, 1889.

CHAPTER 4

1. McDougall's autobiography and archival photos indicate that this shipyard would have been located between the Superwood plant and the present-day BendTec pipe fabrication plant at the corner of Railroad Street and Garfield Avenue.

2. McDougall, *Letter of Recommendation for Robert Clark*, November 23, 1896.

3. Unattributed statement in Beck, "The History and Significance of the S.S. *Meteor*," chap. 3: 1.

4. C. W. Wetmore to American Steel Barge Company Board, *Biographies of Calderwood and Kidd* (Fall 1892).

5. "Added to the Fleet," *Duluth Evening Herald*, July 16, 1889, as quoted by Beck, "The History and Significance of the S.S. *Meteor*," chap. 4: 5.

6. Alexander McDougall to Colgate Hoyt, August 14, 1889.

7. The author witnessed this same equipment and procedure used as late as 1992 to bend heavy wall pipe. It requires a highly skilled well-coordinated team.

8. Daley, "'Pigs' on the Water," 38.

9. Babcock, "System of Work in a Great Lakes Shipyard."

10. Abell, *The Shipwright's Trade*, 139.

11. Ibid., 139.

12. Clark, "The Advent of the Whalebacks on the Great Lakes," *Nor'easter* 23, no. 5 (September–October).

13. Crisman, *Coffin of the Brave Lake Shipwrecks of the War of 1812*, 170. Crisman reports that convex glass deck lights of this type were first patented in England in 1807.

14. Alexander McDougall to Colgate Hoyt, August 14, 1889.

15. McDougall, "Account Book."

16. Gilmore, *The St. Lawrence River Canals Vessel*.

17. McDougall, "Account Book."

18. American Steel Barge Company—relative earnings of the different boats engaged in the Lake Superior trade compared with our own vessels; probably McDougall, late 1891, early 1892.

19. Alexander McDougall to Hoyt, August 14, 1889.

20. Ibid. When McDougall refers to "1,500 tons" or "tons capacity," he means "registered tons"—a legal measurement of the vessel's internal volume in cubic feet divided by 100 tons/cubic foot, not the vessel's actual cargo carrying capacity.

21. For a selection of these silly remarks, see McDougall, *Autobiography of Captain Alexander McDougall*, 32.

22. William Wallace Bates was another larger-than-life figure in the development of the Great Lakes shipping industry. A native of the Canadian Maritime Provinces, he moved to Manitowoc, Wisconsin, from Maine where he had learned the shipbuilding trade. During the 1850s in partnership with his father, he built wooden sailing vessels that were famous for remarkably swift passages. His *Clipper City* averaged 18 mph (faster than the *Colgate Hoyt*) on a 90-mile passage under sail. He later joined noted East Coast naval architect John Griffiths in publishing the *U.S. Nautical Magazine*. A review of *Barge 102*'s design by such an authority would have been a "big deal." See Chapelle, *Search for Speed*, 387–89.

23. Alexander McDougall to Colgate Hoyt, August 14, 1889.

24. Weaver, *Resistance and Flow Data for a Whaleback Steamer Hull Form, Model 4760*.

25. McDougall, "Account Book."

26. Gilmore, *The St. Lawrence River Canals Vessel*.

27. Alexander McDougall to Colgate Hoyt, August 14, 1889.

28. Alexander McDougall to C. W. Wetmore, February 5, 1889.

29. McDougall, "Account Book"; Bowling Green State University, *Great Lakes Vessels On-line Index*, Historical Collections of the Great Lakes, Bowling Green State University, available at www.bgsu.edu/cgi-bin/xvs12.cgi.

30. McDougall, *U.S. Patent 429,468*, June 3, 1890.

31. Clark, "The Advent of the Whalebacks on the Great Lakes," *Nor'easter* 23, no. 5 (September–October).

32. "Rudder Failure," *Marine Review*, 1893.

33. Clark, "The Advent of the Whalebacks on the Great Lakes," *Nor'easter* 23, no. 5 (September–October).

34. *Superior Daily Call*, Superior, Wisconsin, October 3, 1890.

35. Varian, *Observations of the Development of Great Lakes Vessels*.

36. Ratios of tonnage vs. cargo capacity is useful for comparing different ships because gross tonnage (one measured ton is 100 cu. ft.) is proportional to the ship's overall volume—what the owner pays for. Cargo capacity is what the owner gets for his money. In the case of iron ore, this capacity would be measured in long tons of 2,240 lbs. when hauling ore.

37. *Duluth Daily News*, Duluth, Minnesota, February 8, 1890.

38. Van Der Linden, *Great Lakes Ships We Remember*, II: 387.

39. Thompson, *Queen of the Lakes*, 34.

CHAPTER 5

1. Thro, *Roster of Whaleback Ships*. Some authors including Thro state that *Barge 107* was constructed in West Superior. ASB records prove otherwise. In particular, the Superior Public Museum collection includes a souvenir invitation for the November twin launch of the steamship *Joseph Colby* (hull 108) and *Barge 109* identifying these as the first vessels built in the new West Superior yard.

2. American Steel Barge Company, *Statement of Ore Shipped During the Season "1890,"* American Steel Barge Company Financial Records.

3. Author's personal experience.

4. McDougall, *Autobiography of Captain Alexander McDougall*, 33.

5. McDougall, *Autobiography of Captain Alexander McDougall*, 34; Wright, *Freshwater Whales*, 45.

6. McDougall, *Autobiography of Captain Alexander McDougall*, 34.

7. Harkins, "American Steel Barge Company," Untitled Timeline, American Steel Barge Folder, Lake Superior Maritime Collection, University of Wisconsin Superior. This timeline is believed to have been compiled by Wes R. Harkins for a talk given on February 8, 1963.

8. Ibid.

9. Ibid.

10. Ibid.

11. Ibid.

12. Ibid.

13. Ibid.

14. McCarthy, *Ships Fastenings*, 149.

15. Quoted in ibid., 149.

16. Harkins, "American Steel Barge Company," Untitled Timeline, n.p.

17. Wright, *Freshwater Whales*, 54.

18. C. W. Wetmore to American Steel Barge Company Board, Memorandum, November 1892.

19. Ibid.

20. Ibid.

21. Ida Strong to Ken Thro, February 3, 1987; Letter of Recommendation signed by A. McDougall, November 23, 1892.

22. C. W. Wetmore to American Steel Barge Company Board, Memorandum, November 1892; Harkins, "American Steel Barge Company," Untitled Timeline.

23. Harkins, "American Steel Barge Company," Untitled Timeline.

24. Ibid.

25. Wright, *Freshwater Whales*, 47.

26. For example, see C. W. Wetmore to American Steel Barge Company Board, Memorandum, November 1892.

27. McDougall, "Account Book."
28. *The Eye of the Northwest*, 1892.
29. Gates, *The Chapters of My Life*.
30. Daley, "'Pigs' on the Water," 38; McHenry, *Fredrick T. Gates*, 1.

CHAPTER 6

1. *Great Lakes Vessels Online Index*, Historical Collections of the Great Lakes, Bowling Green State University, available at www.bgsu.edu/cgi-bin/xvs12.cgi.
2. Cost data from McDougall's Account Book.
3. C. W. Wetmore to American Steel Barge Company Board, Memorandum, November 1892.
4. In this case "gross ton" means a "long ton" equal to 2,240 lbs. weight. This bears no relationship to the "gross tonnage" of a ship, a measure of material volume.
5. "Statistics of Lake Commerce," *Marine Review*, 1894.
6. Ibid.
7. American Steel Barge Company, "Financial Statements of Earnings and Expenses for Barges, 1891."
8. Based on the change in Consumer Price Index.
9. American Steel Barge Company Financial Statements of Earnings and Expenses for Barges, 1891, McDougall's Account Book.
10. Today, many "high-tech" growth companies forgo a dividend, investors relying on appreciation of stock value to provide an investment return. This is only possible because of the liquidity of today's publicly traded stocks.

CHAPTER 7

1. Alexander McDougall to Colgate Hoyt, August 14, 1889.
2. Thro, *Roster of Whaleback Barges and Steamships*.
3. McDougall, *Autobiography of Captain Alexander McDougall*, 43; American Steel Barge Company Operating Statistics, 1892, for J. L. Colby, and Barges 109, 110, 201, and 202.
4. McDougall, "Account Book."
5. American Steel Barge Company Financial Statements, "Atlantic Service," November 23, 1891 to August 13, 1892.
6. Ibid.
7. Ibid.
8. Society for Naval Architects and Marine Engineers, *Historical Transactions, American Bureau of Shipping, 1862–1943*.
9. McDougall, *Autobiography of Captain Alexander McDougall*, 43.
10. Gray and Lingwood, *The Doxford Turret Ships*.

11. Thomas, *British Ocean Tramps*, I: 32.

12. Goodall, "Whaleback Steamers," Royal Institute of Naval Architects, April 7, 1892.

13. Dougan, *The History of North East Shipbuilding*, 112; *Transactions of North East Coast Institution of Engineers*, vo1. 11, 1894.

14. McDougall, *Autobiography of Captain Alexander McDougall*, 44, 57.

15. Frew, *"Pigs at Sea,"* 139; The Sunderland Site, available at www.searlecanada.org /Sunderland.

16. Items 968 and 969, Roll 33, *Naval Architectural Drawings*, American Shipbuilding Co. and Predecessors, Historical Collection of the Great Lakes, Bowling Green State University.

17. Thomas, *British Ocean Tramps*, I: 32.

18. American Steel Barge Company, *Cash Flow Projections*, July 1, 1892, September 15, 1892, and November 1, 1892.

19. Undated Announcement, *Marine Review*, probably August/September 1892 based on context of other material on this same copy.

20. American Steel Barge Company, *Cash Flow Projections*, undated but late 1892; American Steel Barge Company, *Ledger Balances*, November 30, 1892.

21. "Contracted for Two," *Duluth Evening Herald*, February 14, 1893.

22. Thomas, *British Ocean Tramps*, I: 33. Thro, *Roster of Whaleback Barges and Steamships*.

23. *Superior Daily Call*, Superior, Wisconsin, April 20, 1891.

24. Doxford Engine Friends Association, available at www.globalmarine.com/directory /1346-doxford_engine_friends_association.

25. McDougall, *Autobiography of Captain Alexander McDougall*, 44.

26. C. W. Wetmore to American Steel Barge Company Board, November 21, 1892. In this letter Wetmore reports that he traveled to West Superior in company with William Johnston.

27. Doxford Engine Friends Association, available at www.globalmarine.com.

28. McDougall, *Autobiography of Captain Alexander McDougall*, 57. McDougall describes a trip to Europe in later years during which he and his daughter were royally entertained by William Johnston.

29. Thomas, *British Ocean Tramps*, I: 34.

30. Waine, *Steam Coasters and Short Sea Traders*, 99; Goodall, "Whaleback Steamers," Royal Institute of Naval Architects, April 7, 1892.

31. Babcock, "System of Work in a Great Lakes Shipyard."

32. American Steel Barge Company, *Operating Statistics*, Atlantic Service Vessels, November 24, 1891, to August 13, 1892. This document contains an entry "Amts Charged Ins. a/c loss of wheel."

33. Goodall, "Whaleback Steamers," Royal Institute of Naval Architects, April 7, 1892.

34. Doxford Engine Friends Association, available at www.globalmarine.com and www .searlecananda.org; "Doxford Turret Ships," available at www.shipnostalga.com; *Transactions of North East Coast Institution of Engineers*, vol. 11, 1894.

35. The first turret ship to be classified by Lloyds was the SS *Bencliff* launched in 1894, *Lloyds Register Info Sheet 40*, Turret Ships, available at www.lr.org/documents.

36. Dougan, *The History of North East Shipbuilding*, 112.

37. Thomas, *British Ocean Tramps*, I: 32.

38. Dougan, *The History of North East Shipbuilding*, 112.

39. www.searlecanada.org.

40. McDougall, *Autobiography of Captain Alexander McDougall*, 42.

41. McDougall, *Autobiography of Captain Alexander McDougall*, 43; Gates, *The Chapters of My Life*.

42. "McDougall's Rudder," *Marine Review*, 1893; American Steel Barge Company, "Chas W. Wetmore, in account with Pacific Steel Barge Company."

43. Pacific Steel Barge Company, *Ledger Balances*, September 30, 1892; McDougall, "Account Book." It appears to have been American Steel Barge's practice to carry all vessels in their fleet at a "market value" instead of cost. As the ship was lost in early September 1892, and presumably insured, the book value of the ship could have netted the company an actual cash profit if the insurers had agreed to insure the vessel for the higher value.

44. Zoss, *McDougall's Great Lakes Whalebacks*, 67; Thro, *Roster of Whaleback Barges and Steamships*.

45. Zoss, *McDougall's Great Lakes Whalebacks*, 98; Thro, *Roster of Whaleback Barges and Steamships*.

46. An unusually complete set of drawings for the ship may be found on microfilm roll 27 in the collection of naval architectural drawings held by Bowling Green State University, Bowling Green, Ohio.

47. McDougall, *Autobiography of Captain Alexander McDougall*, 46; Zoss, *McDougall's Great Lakes Whalebacks*, 99; *City of Everett*, Fr. Dowling S.J., Marine Historical Collection, available at www.dalnet.lib.mi.

48. McDougall, *Autobiography of Captain Alexander McDougall*, 48.

49. Ibid., 43.

50. Zoss, *McDougall's Great Lakes Whalebacks*, 67, 69, 71; Pellett, *The Machinery of the Steamship Meteor*, Table 5.

51. Gardner, *Advent of Steam*, 114.

52. Thomas, *British Ocean Tramps*, I: 32.

CHAPTER 8

1. Thro, *Roster of Whaleback Barges and Steamships*.

2. Wright, *Freshwater Whales*, 54.

3. Harkins, "American Steel Barge Company," Untitled Timeline, American Steel Barge Folder, Lake Superior Maritime Collection, University of Wisconsin Superior. This timeline is believed to have been compiled by Wes R. Harkins for a talk given on February 8, 1963.

4. McDougall, *Autobiography of Captain Alexander McDougall*, 35.

5. Pellett, *Drawings for Whaleback Barges and Steamships.*

6. Conclusive evidence of this can be found on drawing 993, Roll 33 of the whaleback naval architectural drawings from the Bowling Green State University archives. This drawing includes a family of displacement curves—hull displacement plotted against hull draft. There is one curve for a vessel's fore section, another for the after section, and several curves for midsections of different lengths. Adding together displacement for a midsection of specified length with that for the forward and after sections gives displacement for the ship. This system will only work if ships of different overall lengths are built with fore and after sections with the same hull lines.

7. Clark, *Genesis of the Whalebacks on the Great Lakes.*

8. Marine Matters, *Duluth News Tribune*, March 31, 1896.

9. Abell, *The Shipwright's Trade*, 139–40.

10. McDougall, *Frame Work for Vessels*, U.S. Patent 456586, dated April 18, 1890.

11. In his autobiography, Alexander McDougall says that his formal education was very limited and that the little mathematics that he needed for navigation he picked up from captains of ships that he sailed on. Robert Clark's granddaughter, Ida Strong, described him as "self-educated-very little schooling" to whaleback researcher Ken Thro in a May 10, 1987, letter.

12. See Benford, *Naval Architecture for Non-Naval Architects*, chap. 12, for an easily understood introduction to this subject. Benford, a long-time professor at the University of Michigan had the talent to rapidly sketch the outline of a pig over the distorted hull of a ship to demonstrate the concept of "hogging." Unfortunately his book does not include this cartoon.

13. A beam's "section modulus" is a measure of its ability to resist bending forces. The section modulus is a function of the beam size, thickness, and arrangement of materials of construction. Calculation of section moduli for different beams produces an accurate comparison for different beams under the same loading conditions. A ship's hull behaves like a huge beam. To compare the strength of whaleback-shaped hulls with conventional-shaped hulls, section moduli were calculated for differently shaped hulls with the same cross-sectional dimensions. The section modulus for the conventional hull was found to be 28% higher than that for the whaleback.

14. Crothers, *American-Built Packets and Freighters of the 1850s*, 61, 129, 130, 167; Arnott, *Design and Construction of Steel Merchant Ships*, 62.

15. Beck, "The History and Significance of the S.S. *Meteor*," chap. 8: 7.

16. Holms, *Practical Shipbuilding*, Article 33, 24; Arnott, *Design and Construction of Steel Merchant Ships*, 74; True, "60 Years of Shipbuilding."

17. Holms, *Practical Shipbuilding*, Article 32, 23.

18. Holms, *Practical Shipbuilding*, Article 181; Arnott, *Design and Construction of Steel Merchant Ships*, 80, 84.

19. Cross, "Recent Developments in Shipbuilding on the Great Lakes," Society of Naval Architects and Marine Engineers Transactions, 1928.

20. Pellett, *The Machinery of the Steamship* Meteor.

21. Ibid.

22. Ibid.

23. McDougall, *U.S. Patent 468,913*, dated March 1, 1892.

24. "Electric Lighting Plant on the Pillsbury," *Electrical World* 20 (1892).

25. Seibert, "Architectural Accuracy and the Artists," *Inland Seas* 30, no. 2 (1974).

26. "Lack Marine Exhibits," *Marine Review*, bound volume, 1893.

27. The model of the *Frank Rockefeller* in the collection of the Mariners Museum at Newport News, Virginia, was donated to the museum by Alexander McDougall's estate. The construction and workmanship of this model indicates that it was built by the same individual who built a model of the passenger whaleback steamship owned by the Duluth Children's Museum. The Children's Museum claims that their model was built by George Stevens, McDougall's patent attorney (the model is not a patent model). An interesting feature of the Mariners Museum model is its color scheme—it is painted in the old buff turret America Steel Barge color scheme. When the *Frank Rockefeller* was launched in 1896 she was painted with white turrets reflecting the fact that the fleet was now being managed by Pickands Mather. This model may have been built in 1892 or 1893 to demonstrate a new generation of whaleback steamships of which the *Frank Rockefeller* would become the first example.

28. McDougall, *Autobiography of Alexander McDougall*, 34.

29. Pellett, *Drawings for Whaleback Ships*.

30. *Marine Review* 28, no. 8 (1893).

31. C. W. Wetmore to Colgate Hoyt, November 21, 1892; Colgate Hoyt to C. W. Wetmore, December 15, 1892.

32. Bowling Green State University Great Lakes Vessel Data Base.

33. Arnott, *Design and Construction of Steel Merchant Ships*, 30.

34. *Washburn* and *Pillsbury*, Roll 27, Naval Architectural Drawings, American Shipbuilding Co. and Predecessors, Historical Collection of the Great Lakes, Bowling Green State University.

35. Ibid.

36. Hilton, *Lake Michigan Passenger Steamers*, 74.

37. Item 988, Roll 33, Naval Architectural Drawings, American Shipbuilding Co. and Predecessors, Historical Collection of the Great Lakes, Bowling Green State University.

38. Correspondence of American Steel Barge Company from C. W. Wetmore to Colgate Hoyt, November 21, 1892; *Barges 126* and *127*, Roll 27, Naval Architectural Drawings, American Shipbuilding Co. and Predecessors, Historical Collection of the Great Lakes, Bowling Green State University.

39. *Great Lakes Vessels Online Index*, Historical Collections of the Great Lakes, Bowling Green State University, available at www.bgsu.edu/cgi-bin/xvs12.cgi.

40. Financial Analyses of the American Steel Barge Company Steamers, *Pillsbury*, *Washburn*, *Pathfinder*, and *Barge Sagamore*.

41. McDougall, *U.S. Patent 500,411*, dated June 27, 1893.

42. Ibid.

43. Hilton, *Lake Michigan Passenger Steamers*, 61, 73, 88, 89; Gardner, *Advent of Steam: The Ship, 1900–1060*, chap. 3.

44. McDougall. *The Autobiography of Alexander McDougall*, 38.

45. *Great Lakes Vessels Online Index*, Historical Collections of the Great Lakes, Bowling Green State University, available at www.bgsu.edu/cgi-bin/xvs12.cgi; McDougall, "Account Book."

46. Hilton, *Lake Michigan Passenger Steamers*, 94.

47. American Steel Barge Company, Colgate Hoyt to C. W. Wetmore, December 15, 1892.

48. *Chicago Tribune*, May 18, 1893, quoted in McDougall, *Autobiography of Captain Alexander McDougall*, 35.

49. McDougall, "Account Book."

50. Hilton, *Lake Michigan Passenger Steamers*, 265–67.

CHAPTER 9

1. Walker, "The Mesabe Range Goes to Market," chap. 5. *Iron Frontier*, Minnesota Historical Society Press, 1979.

2. Walker, *Iron Frontier*, 112; McDougall, *The Autobiography of Captain Alexander McDougall*, 40.

3. Harrison, *Prominent and Progressive Americans*, "Charles W. Wetmore," vol. 2.

4. Walker, *Iron Frontier*, 113; Charles W. Wetmore to Colgate Hoyt, November 21, 1892.

5. Charles W. Wetmore to Colgate Hoyt, November 21, 1892.

6. McDougall, *Autobiography of Captain Alexander McDougall*, 42.

7. Colgate Hoyt to Charles W. Wetmore, December 15, 1892.

8. Charles W. Wetmore to Colgate Hoyt, November 21, 1892.

9. Ibid.

10. Ibid.

11. Gates's abrasive personality comes across in his autobiography, *The Chapters in My Life*.

12. American Steel Barge Company, Cash Flow Projections, July 1, 1892, November 1, 1892.

13. Ibid.

14. McDougall, "Account Book."

15. American Steel Barge Company, Cash Flow Projection, November 1, 1892.

16. Ibid.

17. Charles W. Wetmore to Colgate Hoyt, November 21, 1892.

18. Colgate Hoyt to American Steel Barge Company Shareholders, December 14, 1892.

19. Wright, *Iron Frontier*, 47; Daley, "'Pigs' on the Water," 56.

20. American Steel Barge Company to the Farmers Loan and Trust Company, *Mortgage*, Douglas County, Wisconsin: Mortgage Record 28: June 6, 1893.

21. Walker, *Iron Frontier*, 139.
22. Ibid., 383. This tells how John D. Rockefeller was able to control the Merritt brothers' iron ore holdings while owning a minority interest of less than 20% of the stock. He did this by holding a mortgage on their properties.
23. Fell, "Rockefeller's Right Hand Man: Fredrick T. Gates and the Northwestern Mining Investments," *Business History Review*, 546.
24. Thro, *Roster of Whaleback Barges and Steamships*.
25. Ibid.
26. American Steel Barge Company, *Directors Minutes*, February 23, 1893.
27. McDougall, *Autobiography of Captain Alexander McDougall*, 42.
28. Ibid., 47, 48.
29. Ibid., 47.
30. Misa, *Nation of Steel*, 159; Daley, "'Pigs' on the Water," 6.
31. Chernow, *Titan*, 110.
32. http://www.ohiohistorycentral.org/w/Panic_of_1893.
33. "Statistics of Lake Commerce," *Marine Review*, 1894.
34. Entry 950, Roll 33, Naval Architectural Drawings, American Shipbuilding Co. and Predecessors, Historical Collection of the Great Lakes, Bowling Green State University.
35. Thro, *Roster of Whaleback Barges and Steamships*.
36. Fell, "Rockefeller's Right Hand Man: Fredrick T. Gates and the Northwestern Mining Investments," *Business History Review*, no. 4 (1978): 546.
37. McDougall, *Autobiography of Captain Alexander McDougall*, 48.
38. Zoss, *McDougall's Great Lakes Whalebacks*, 56.
39. Hilton, *Lake Michigan Passenger Steamers*, 265–67; *Great Lakes Vessels Online Index*, Historical Collections of the Great Lakes, Bowling Green State University, available at www.bgsu.edu/cgi-bin/xvs12.cgi.
40. *Great Lakes Vessels Online Index*, Historical Collections of the Great Lakes, Bowling Green State University, available at www.bgsu.edu/cgi-bin/xvs12.cgi; "Big Whaleback Coaster," *New York Times*, April 30, 1900.
41. Havinghurst, *Vein of Iron*, 92.
42. Purves, *John H. Roes Steamship Company*, 56.
43. Walker, *Iron Frontier*, 115.
44. Ibid., 140, 141.
45. Ibid., 140.
46. Ibid., 147.
47. Ibid., 147.
48. Ibid., 288; Charles W. Wetmore to Colgate Hoyt, November 21, 1892.
49. Wright, *Iron Frontier*, 51.
50. McDougall, *Autobiography of Captain Alexander McDougall*, 48.
51. Walker, *Iron Frontier*, 178.

52. Wright, *Freshwater Whales*, 51.

53. Daley, "'Pigs' on the Water," 60.

54. Wright, *Freshwater Whales*, 137.

55. McDougall, *Letter of Recommendation for Robert Clark*, November 23, 1896.

56. McDougall, *Autobiography of Captain Alexander McDougall*, 48.

57. Daley, "'Pigs' on the Water," 61.

58. McDougall, *Autobiography of Captain Alexander McDougall*, 48.

59. http://rockefeller100.0rg/biography/show/fredrick-t-gates.

CHAPTER 10

1. "Great Trade in Iron Ore," *New York Times*, December 16, 1896.

2. Miller, *Tin Stackers*, 2.

3. "Great Lakes Vessel Database," *Marine Review*, April 23, 1896.

4. Chernow, *Titan*, 110. Although this passage refers to Rockefeller's oil operations, the circumstances apply equally to his iron ore business.

5. Babcock, "System of Work in a Great Lakes Shipyard."

6. "A New Whaleback," *Duluth News Tribune*, October 5, 1895.

7. Daley, "'Pigs' on the Water," 58.

8. American Steel Barge Company vessel comparison. Although undated, whaleback historian Mathew Daley identifies this document found in American Steel Barge files as having been authored by McDougall or possibly Hoyt. I believe that it was written by McDougall as it is very similar to a talk that McDougall gave in Chicago about the same time.

9. Determination of bending moment for a ship's hull in a seaway is a complex calculation with results dependent on the shape of the ship's hull, buoyancy distribution, distribution of weight, and size and amplitude of waves. For a rectangular beam with distributed load, the maximum bending moment is a function of the square of the beam's length. Therefore, to the extent that a ship represents a beam with distributed load, the bending moment for a 400 ft. ship is 2.8 times, not 1.57 times that of a 240 ft. vessel. This assumption that bending moment varies by the square of the ship's length is reflected in classification society and load line rules.

10. "Took in the Launch," *Duluth Evening Herald*, April 27, 1896. There is a local legend that Franklin D. Roosevelt attended the launch, arriving aboard a special train from the East. If this is true, and no evidence to substantiate it has been found, he would have been fourteen years old.

11. *American Society of Naval Engineers Transactions*, 1896.

12. Naval Architectural Drawings, American Shipbuilding Co. and Predecessors, Historical Collection of the Great Lakes, Bowling Green State University, *Hull 136*.

13. Ibid.

14. Ibid.

15. See Arnott, *Design and Construction of Steel Merchant Ships*, chap. 3: A, for a history of iron and steel ship structural design including structural section midship drawings for representative Great Lakes ships.

16. Naval Architectural Drawings, American Shipbuilding Co. and Predecessors, Historical Collection of the Great Lakes, Bowling Green State University, *Hull 136*.

17. Abell, *The Shipwright's Trade*, 138.

18. Pellett, *The Machinery of the Steamship Meteor*.

19. Thro, *Roster of Whaleback Ships*.

20. Havinghurst, *Vein of Iron*, 92. The model of the *Frank Rockefeller* in the collection of the Mariners Museum in Newport News, Virginia, and mentioned earlier is painted in the colors of the American Steel Barge Company.

21. Thro, *Roster of Whaleback Ships*.

22. *Marine Review*, April 23, 1896.

23. Block coefficient is the ratio of the underwater volume of a ship to the volume of a rectangular block, the dimensions of which are the length, draft, and beam. The relationship is expressed as a decimal. Benford, *Naval Architecture*, 204.

24. Naval Architectural Drawings, American Shipbuilding Co. and Predecessors, Historical Collection of the Great Lakes, Bowling Green State University, *Hull 141*. *Mauna Loa* drawings are attached to Babcock, "System of Work in a Great Lakes Shipyard."

25. Pellett, *Machinery of the Steamship Meteor*.

26. "The Greatest of the Whalebacks," *Minneapolis Journal*, December 31, 1898.

27. The *Christopher Columbus*, English *Sagamore*, and the *City of Everett* are not included in the thirty-five vessel statistics.

28. The fates of these five "third generation." Thro, *Roster of Whaleback Ships*, and Zoss, *McDougall's Great Lakes Whalebacks*.

CONCLUSION

1. *Barges 104* and *115* were blown ashore after losing their tows. *Barge 129* sank after colliding with the towing vessel, the steamship *Thomas Wilson* sank after colliding with another vessel, and the *Sagamore* sank after colliding with another vessel. See Zoss, *McDougall's Great Lakes Whalebacks*, for a brief summary of the fate of each whaleback vessel.

2. Lafferty and Van Heest, *Buckets and Belts*, includes several chapters discussing Latham D. Smith and his tunnel scraper self-unloading system that may have contributed to the loss of the converted whaleback steamship *Clifton*.

3. Fates of whaleback barges were tabulated from information provided in Zoss, *McDougall's Great Lakes Whalebacks*, and Thro, *Roster of Whaleback Ships*.

4. "Tells Story of the Movement of Whalebacks," *Amherstburg Echo*, Amherstburg Ontario, Canada, August 11, 1956. Ships are designed to specific requirements of owners who do not wish to pay for features not required by the ship's particular trade. Unfor-

tunately this does not prevent the vessel from being used later in its life for a purpose for which it was not designed, sometimes with tragic results. An example is the *Benjamin Noble*. Designed to haul a light buoyant cargo of pulpwood, she foundered in a gale on Lake Superior loaded with a heavy cargo of railroad rails.

5. Present-day authors Zoss, *McDougall's Great Lakes Whalebacks*, 9, and Bowlus, *Iron Ore Transport on the Great Lakes*, 159, make this argument.

6. Arnott, *Design and Construction of Steel Merchant Ships*, chap. 3: A.

7. Naval Architectural Drawings, American Shipbuilding Co. and Predecessors, Historical Collection of the Great Lakes, Bowling Green State University. Although most were removed in 1943 during her conversion to a tanker, one of the large structural arches added to permit removal of internal hold beams and stanchions still exists aboard the SS *Meteor* (*Frank Rockefeller*).

8. Barnes, "Brief History of Riverside Shipyard," *McDougall Scrap Book and Photo Album*.

9. "Statistics of Lake Commerce," *Marine Review*, 1894; *Operating Revenues and Costs for 1891*, American Steel Barge Company.

10. Clark, *The Advent of the Whaleback Ship*.

11. Thompson, *An Ancient Mariner Reflects*, 46.

12. Naval Architectural Drawings, American Shipbuilding Co. and Predecessors, Historical Collection of the Great Lakes, Bowling Green State University. Some authors including the National Park Service website for the sunken whaleback steamship *Thomas Wilson* have claimed that the later whalebacks were built with hatches set in raised coamings, but this is not true. Design drawings and archival photographs both show that all whaleback barges and steamships were originally built with Alexander McDougall's flush plate hatch system. For example, see Zoss, *McDougall's Great Lakes Whalebacks*, 108.

13. Boyer, *Great Stories of the Great Lakes*, chap. 8; Thompson, *Graveyard of the Lakes*.

14. Meakin, *Master of the Inland Seas*, 105. The invention required to make these heavy steel hatch covers work was a traveling gantry crane small enough to fit on the ship's deck and lightweight enough not to affect stability. Powering such a device with steam was not practical, and development of the electric induction motor was in its infancy. When compact electric induction motors had been developed, the hatch gantry crane became a reality.

15. Benford, *The Great Storm of 1913*.

16. Wright, *Freshwater Whales*, 52.

17. Lenihan, *Shipwrecks of Isle Royal National Park*, 35.

18. For an account of the steady growth in the size of lake freighters, see Thompson, *Queen of the Lakes*.

19. Bowlus, *Iron Ore Transport on the Great Lakes*, 175, 189. Miller, *Tin Stackers*, 39, discusses this topic as it applied to the Pittsburgh Steamship, a successor organization.

20. Miller, *Tin Stackers*, 40.

EPILOGUE

1. For the merger of the American Steel Barge Company into the American Shipbuilding Company, see Wright, *Freshwater Whales*, chap. 7.
2. *Marine Review*, May 18, 1899.
3. McDougall, *Autobiography of Captain Alexander McDougall*, 48; *Marine Review*, September 11, 1899.
4. McDougall, *Autobiography of Captain Alexander McDougall*, 51–67.
5. Daley, "Duluth's Other Company Town: The McDougall-Duluth Company, Riverside, World War I Shipping." *Minnesota History* (Spring 2013).
6. McDougall, *Autobiography of Captain Alexander McDougall*, 74.
7. This house, beautifully maintained, still stands. McDougall's grave is in Duluth's Forest Hill Cemetery, and the retreat that he loved on Wisconsin's Brule River is still owned by his family.
8. Wright, *Freshwater Whales*, 51. Wright erroneously refers to Robert as James Clark.
9. American Steel Barge Company, McDougall to "Whom it May Concern," November 23, 1896.
10. Ida Strong to Ken Thro, February 3, 1987.
11. *Marine Review*, April 29, 1897.
12. *Marine Record*, February 24, 1898, and September 7, 1899.
13. *Blue Book of American Shipping, 1903*. Duluth's Board of Trade Building still stands, occupied by modern offices. The Minnesota Ballet practices in the large room where grain futures were once traded. The large boards where prices were posted still surround the room.
14. Frew, *"Pigs at Sea,"* 138.
15. *Marine Record*, February 8, 1900.
16. *Marine Review*, September 19, 1901.
17. Wright, *Freshwater Whales*, 140.
18. *Marine Review*, January 24, 1895.
19. *Buffalo Evening News*, July 22, 1905.
20. *Great Lakes Vessels Online Index*, Historical Collections of the Great Lakes, Bowling Green State University, available at www.bgsu.edu/cgi-bin/xvs12.cgi; Thro, *Roster of Whaleback Ships*.
21. Daniel, *Shipwrecks along Lake Superior's North Shore*, 26.
22. "Sell Off Its Small Boats," *Detroit Free Press*, November 1, 1904.
23. Snow and Lee, *A Shipyard in Maine*, 268.
24. Both Thro, *Roster of Whaleback Ships*, and Zoss, *McDougall's Great Lakes Whalebacks*, provide information about these whaleback tankers.
25. Pittsburgh Steamship's modernization program may be tracked by analyzing the large number of available archive photographs in conjunction with the Bowling Green State University drawings.

26. For disposal of whaleback vessels, see Miller, *Tin Stackers*, appendices 2 and 3. For subsequent careers, see Zoss, *McDougall's Great Lakes Whalebacks.*

27. Zoss, *McDougall's Great Lakes Whalebacks*, 49–55, 104–27. See also *Great Lakes Vessels Online Index*, Historical Collections of the Great Lakes, Bowling Green State University, available at www.bgsu.edu/cgi-bin/xvs12.cgi, for ownership changes.

28. U.S. Coast Guard Report, November 22, 1969.

29. Wright, *Freshwater Whales*, 53.

30. Harkins, "American Steel Barge Company," Untitled Timeline.

31. Thompson, *Queen of the Lakes*, 102.

32. Lapinski, "In the Yard," April 14, 2004.

33. Ibid.

BIBLIOGRAPHY

BOOKS

Abell, Sir Wescott. *The Shipwright's Trade.* London: Conway Maritime Press, 1948.

Anon. *Marine Boilers and Refrigeration: International Library of Technology.* International Text Book Company, 1907.

Arnott, David, ed. *Design and Construction of Steel Merchant Ships.* New York: Society of Naval Architects and Marine Engineers, 1955.

Attwood, E. L., and I. C. G. Cooper. *A Text Book of Laying Off: Or the Geometry of Shipbuilding.* London: Longmans, Green and Co., 1938.

Benford, Harry. *Naval Architecture for Non-Naval Architects.* Jersey City, NJ: Society of Naval Architects and Marine Engineers, 2006.

Bowlus, W. Bruce. *Iron Ore Transport on the Great Lakes.* Jefferson, NC: McFarland & Co., 2010.

Boyer, Dwight. *Great Stories of the Great Lakes.* New York: Dodd, Mead, and Company, 1966.

Chapelle, Howard I. *The Search for Speed under Sail.* New York: Bonanza Books, 1967.

Chernow, Ron. *Titan: The Life of John D. Rockefeller.* New York: Random House, 1998.

Corlett, Ewan. *The Iron Ship: The History and Significance of Brunel's Great Britain.* Bradford-on-Avon, Wiltshire: Moonraker Press, 1980.

Crisman, Kevin J., ed. *Coffins of the Brave Lake Shipwrecks of the War of 1812.* College Station: Texas A&M University Press, 2014.

Crothers, *American-Built Packets and Freighters of the 1850s: An Illustrated Study of Their Characteristics and Construction.* Jefferson, NC: McFarland & Company, 2013.

Curr, Robert. *Lake Shipyard Methods of Steel Ship Construction.* Cleveland, OH: The Marine Review, 1907.

Daniel, Stephen B. *Shipwrecks along Lake Superior's North Shore.* St. Paul: Minnesota Historical Society Press, 2008.

Dougan, David. *The History of North East Shipbuilding.* London: George Allen and Unwin, 1968.

Frew, David. *Pigs at Sea: The Sinking of the James B. Colgate.* Erie, PA: Erie County Historical Society, 2008.

Gardiner, Robert, ed. *The Advent of Steam: The Ship.* London: Conway Maritime Press, 1994.

Gardiner, Robert, ed., *The Golden Age of Shipping: The Ship, 1900–1960.* London: Conway Maritime Press. 1994.

Garzke, William H., and John B. Woodward. *Titanic Ships, Titanic Disasters: An Analysis of Early Cunard and White Star Superliners.* Jersey City, NJ: Society of Naval Architects and Marine Engineers, 2002.

Gates, Fredrick T. *The Chapters in My Life.* New York: Free Press, 1977.

Gray, Leonard, and John Lingwood. *The Doxford Turret Ships.* McDenna, UK: World Ship Society, 1975.

Havinghurst, Walter. *Vein of Iron: The Pickands Mather Story.* Cleveland, OH: World Publishing Co., 1958.

Herreshoff, L. Francis, Cpt. *Nat Herreshoff: His Life and the Yachts He Designed.* New York: Sheridan House, 1974.

Hilton, George W. *Lake Michigan Passenger Steamers.* Stanford, CA: Stanford University Press, 2002.

Holms, A. Campbell. *Practical Shipbuilding,* 2 vols. London: Longmans, Green and Co., 1916.

King, Frank A. *The Mesabi Road.* Minneapolis: University of Minnesota Press, 2003.

Lafferty, William, and Valerie Van Heest. *Buckets and Belts, Evolution of the Great Lakes Self Unloader.* Holland, MI: In Depth Editions, 2009.

Lenihan, Daniel J. *Shipwrecks of Isle Royal National Park.* Duluth, MN: Lake Superior Port Cities, 1994.

McCarthy Michael. *Ships Fastenings: From Sewn Boat to Steamship.* College Station: Texas A&M University Press, 2005.

McDougall, Alexander. *The Autobiography of Captain Alexander McDougall.* Cleveland, OH: The Great Lakes Historical Society, 1968.

Meakin, Alexander. *Master of the Inland Seas: The Story of Captain Thomas Wilson and the Fleet That Bore His Name.* Vermillion, OH: The Great Lakes Historical Society, 1988.

Miller, Al. *Tin Stackers: The History of the Pittsburgh Steamship Company.* Detroit, MI: Wayne State University Press, 1999.

Misa, Thomas J. *A Nation of Steel.* Baltimore, MD: Johns Hopkins University Press, 1995.

Purves, John H. *Roen Steamship Company: The Way It Was, 1909–1976.* Sturgeon Bay, WI: Door County Maritime Museum, 1983.

Rodgers, Bradley A. *Guardian of the Lakes: The U.S. Paddle Frigate Michigan.* Ann Arbor: University of Michigan Press, 1968.

Rossell, Henry E., and Lawrence B. Chapman, eds. *Principles of Naval Architecture.* New York: Society of Naval Architects and Marine Engineers, 1962.

Snow, Ralph Linwood, and Cpt. Douglas K. Lee. *A Shipyard in Maine: Percy Small and the Great Schooners.* Gardner, ME: Tilbury House, 2005.

Thiesen, William H. *Industrializing American Shipbuilding: The Transformation of Ship Design and Construction, 1820–1920.* Gainesville: University Press of Florida, 2006.

Thomas, P. N. *British Ocean Tramps: Builders and Cargoes,* vols. 1 and 2. Merchant steam series. Albrighton, Wolverhampton: Waine Research, 1992.

Thompson, Mark L. *Graveyard of the Lakes.* Detroit, MI: Wayne State University Press, 2000.

Thompson, Mark L. *Queen of the Lakes.* Detroit, MI: Wayne State University Press, 1994.

Thompson, Cpt. Merwin Stone. *An Ancient Mariner Recollects.* Oxford, OH: Typoprint, c. 1967.

Van Der Linden, Rev. Peter. *Great Lakes Ships We Remember,* 3 vols. Detroit, MI: Marine Historical Society of Detroit, 1984.

Waine, Charles V. *Steam Coasters and Short Sea Traders.* Wolverhampton: Waine Research Publications, 1980.

Walker, David A. *Iron Frontier: The Discovery and Development of Minnesota's Iron Range.* St. Paul: Minnesota Historical Society Press, 2004.

Walker, Fred. *Ships and Shipbuilders:* Annapolis, MD: US Naval Institute Press, 2010.

Wright, Richard J. *Freshwater Whales: The History of the American Shipbuilding Company and Its Predecessors.* Kent, OH: Kent State University Press, 1969.

Zoss, Neel R. *McDougall's Great Lakes Whalebacks.* Charleston, SC: Arcadia Publishing, 2007.

CLASSIFICATION SOCIETY REGISTERS

Blue Book of American Shipping: Marine and Naval Directory of the United States; Statistics of Shipping and Shipbuilding in America. Cleveland, OH: Marine Review Publishing Co., 1896–1903.

Great Lakes Register, Steam Vessels 1899, American Shipmasters Association.

Great Lakes Register, Steam Vessels 1913. American Shipmasters Association.

Mitchell & Company's Hand Book of the Great Lakes. Cleveland, OH: Mitchell & Co., 1913.

The Standard American Classification of Shipping. Cleveland, OH: American Bureau of Shipping, Great Lakes Department, 1927.

The Standard American Classification of Shipping. Cleveland, OH: American Bureau of Shipping, Great Lakes Department, 1932.

PAPERS AND JOURNAL ARTICLES

Babcock, W. I. "System of Work in a Great Lakes Shipyard." *Society of Naval Architects and Marine Engineers Transactions*, 1898.

Benford, Harry. "The Great Storm of 1913: Up Close and Personal." Paper presented to the Great Lakes and Great Rivers Section, Society of Naval Architects and Marine Engineers, May 13, 2005.

Bennett, William. "Great Lakes Bulk Freighters." *Society of Naval Architects and Marine Engineers Transactions*, 1929.

Burke, John A. "Barrels to Barrows, Buckets to Belts: 120 Years of Iron Ore Handling on the Great Lakes." Paper presented at the annual meeting of the Great Lakes Historical Society, 1975. (Later published in Great Lakes Historical Society journal *Inland Seas.*)

Cross, A. W. "Recent Developments in Shipbuilding on the Great Lakes." *Society of Naval Architects and Marine Engineers Transactions*, 1928.

Daley, Matthew L. "Duluth's Other Company Town: The McDougall-Duluth Company, Riverside, and World War I Shipbuilding." *Minnesota History* (Spring 2013).

Fell, James E., Jr. "Rockefeller's Right Hand Man: Fredrick T. Gates and the Northwestern Mining Investments." *Business History Review* 52, no. 4 (1978). Original copyright: Cambridge, MA: The President and Fellows of Harvard College.

Gilmore, James. "The Saint Lawrence River Canal Vessel." *Society of Naval Architects and Marine Engineers Transactions*, 1957.

Goodall, F. C. "Whaleback Steamers." Royal Institute of Naval Architects, April 7, 1892.

Kendall, S. O. "Doxford Turret Ships." *Transactions of the N.E. Coast Institute of Engineers and Shipbuilders* 2, (1894).

Luckenbach, J. Lewis. "American Bureau of Shipping 1862–1943." *Society of Naval Architects and Marine Engineers: Historical Transactions (1893–1943)*, 1945.

Nichols, John F. "The Development of Marine Engineering." *Society of Naval Architects and Marine Engineers, Historical Transactions (1893–1943)*, 1945.

Pellett, C. Roger. "Drawings for Whaleback Barges and Steamships." *Nautical Research Journal* 52, no. 3 (2007).

Sibert, C. Thomas. "Architectural Accuracy and the Artists," *Inland Seas* 30, no. 2 (1974): 95–109.

True, Dwight. "Sixty Years of Shipbuilding." Paper presented to Great Lakes Section, Society of Naval Architects and Marine Engineers, October 5, 1956.

Varian, Howard, "Observations on the Development of Great Lakes Vessels." Address to University of Michigan Quarterdeck Society, May 26, 1956.

Workman, James C. "Shipping on the Great Lakes." *Society of Naval Architects and Marine Engineers, Historical Transactions (1893–1943)*, 1945.

INTERNET RESOURCES

Biography: Lamont Henry Bowers, 1847–1941, http://library.binghamton.edu/special /findingaids/lmbowers_m3.html.

Brief History of the Welland Canal, www.wellandcanal.com.

Dowling, Fr. S.J, Marine Historical Collection, University of Detroit, Mercy, MI, www .dalnet.lib.mi.us/gsdl/cgi-bin/library.

Doxford Engine Friends Association, www.globalmarine.com/directory/1346-doxford _engine_friends_association.

Fredrick T. Gates, 100 Years, The Rockefeller Foundation, www.rockefeller100.org /biography/show/fredrick-t—gates.

Great Lakes Vessels Online Index, Historical Collections of the Great Lakes, Bowling Green State University, www.bgsu.edu/cgi-bin/xvs12.cgi (Great Lakes Vessel Database).

Maritime History of the Great Lakes, www.maritimehistoryofthegreatlakes.ca (of particular value is this website's collection of scanned copies of *Marine Record* and *Marine Review*).

Panic of 1893, Ohio History Central- A product of the Ohio Historical Society, www .ohiohistorycentral.org/w/Panic-of-1893.

Statistics of Lake Commerce, Some Average Lake Freight Rates, www.halinet.on.ca/scripts /Page.asp?PageID=4068.

The Sunderland Site, www.searlecanada.org/sunderland.

Winslow, Scott J. Associates, Inc. Americana, "Colgate Hoyt," www.scottwindslow.com /manufacturer/Hoyt/Colgate/2900.

U.S. PATENTS

McDougall, Alexander. Covering for false bottoms of vessels. Patent 480823, filed Sep. 17, 1891, and issued Aug. 16, 1892.

McDougall, Alexander. Dead-Light. Patent 469913, filed May 22, 1891, and issued Mar. 1, 1892.

McDougall, Alexander. Frame-Work for Vessels. Patent 456586, filed Apr. 19, 1890, and issued July 28, 1891.

McDougall, Alexander. Hawser and anchor-Chain Fair-Leader. Patent 512209, filed Oct. 26, 1892, and issued Jan. 2, 1894.

McDougall, Alexander. Jury-Mast. Patent 456587, filed Sep.12, 1890, and issued July 28, 1891.

McDougall, Alexander. Rudder. Patent 492873, filed Sep. 17, 1891, and issued March 7, 1893.

McDougall, Alexander. Steam Passenger-Boat. Patent 500411, filed Mar. 23, 1891, and issued June 27, 1893.

McDougall, Alexander. Tow Boat. Patent 241813, filed Mar. 9, 1880, and issued May 24, 1881.

McDougall, Alexander. Tow Boat. Patent 259889, filed Apr. 4, 1882, and issued June 20, 1882.

McDougall, Alexander. Tow Boat. Patent 393997, filed Apr. 18, 1888, and issued Dec. 4, 1888.

McDougall, Alexander. Vessel. Patent 489681, filed July 29, 1892, and issued May 30, 1893.

McDougall, Alexander, and the American Steel Barge Company. Anchor. Patent 445816, filed Mar. 24, 1890, and issued Feb. 3, 1891.

McDougall, Alexander, and the American Steel Barge Company. Steam Tow Boat. Patent 429468, filed Sep. 20, 1889, and issued June 3, 1890.

McDougall, Alexander, and the American Steel Barge Company. Tow Boat. Patent 429467, filed May 24, 1889, and issued June 3, 1890.

Note: This list is not inclusive of all patents or all patents for whaleback ships issued to Alexander McDougall. Only those patents relevant to this study are included.

UNPUBLISHED REPORTS

Beck, Bill. "The History and Significance of the S.S. *Meteor.*" (Report Commissioned by Superior Public Museums, June 7, 2007.)

Daley, Matthew L. "'Pigs' on the Water: Technological Failure and Great Lakes Shipbuilding Innovation, 1880–1905" (MA thesis, Wayne State University, 2000).

Harkins, W. R. "American Steel Barge Company: Timeline for West Superior Shipyard." (Undated but believed to be February 8, 1963.)

Lapinski, Patrick. "In the Yard: The History of the Fraser Shipyards, 1945–2000." (Short Version. April 14, 2004.)

McHenry Misha. "Fredrick T. Gates: The Man Behind John D. Rockefeller." (Honors Thesis, Ball State University, 2006.)

Pellett, C. Roger. "The Machinery of the Steamship *Meteor.*" (Unpublished report by Superior Public Museums, October 31, 2006.)

Weaver, A. H., Jr. "Resistance and Flow Data for a Whaleback Steamer Hull Form, Model 4760." (Report 1449, Department of the Navy, David Taylor Model Basin, September 1960.)

PERIODICALS

"Big Whaleback Coaster," *New York Times*, April 30, 1900.

Buffalo Evening News, July 22, 1905.

"Contracted for Two," *Duluth Evening Herald*, February 14, 1893.

"Electric Lighting Plant on the Pillsbury," *Electrical World* 2, no. 24, (1892): 20.

"The Eye of the Northwest," Report of the City Statistician for 1892." City of Superior, Superior, Wisconsin.

"Great Trade in Iron Ore," *New York Times*, December 16, 1896.

"The Greatest of the Whalebacks," *Minneapolis Journal*, December 31, 1898.

"His Fourth Launch, This is McDougall's Day," *Duluth Daily News*, February 8, 1890.

Marine Review, various articles and issues per attribution.

Marine Record, various articles and issues per attribution.

"Sell Off Its Small Boats," *Detroit Free Press*, November 1, 1904.

ARCHIVAL MATERIALS

Drawings: Drawings for ships built by the American Steel Barge Co. and its successor, the American Shipbuilding Co., are held in the collection of the Center for Archival Collections at Bowling Green State University, Bowling Green Ohio. For a complete discussion of this topic, see C. Roger Pellett, Drawings for Whaleback Barges and Steamships listed above.

All drawings are organized under the heading of American Shipbuilding Company and Predecessors—Naval Architectural Drawings have been copied onto two microfilm rolls.

Roll 27 contains drawings for whaleback barges and steamships that were built. Roll 33 generally contains proposed whaleback barges and steamships and miscellaneous design studies, although drawings for *Barge 101* are included on this microfilm roll. Where these drawings apply to the text, the vessel's name or hull number and microfilm roll number is listed in the note.

MANUSCRIPTS

Barnes, Julius. "Brief History of Riverside Shipyard" (a typed unsigned two-page manuscript found by a local resident cleaning out boxes of "junk" from unused buildings at the site of McDougall's WWI-era Riverside Shipyard. Duluth, MN, April 2, 1951).

Clarke, Robert. "Whalebacks There [*sic*] Origin and Advent on the Great Lakes." (Later published in shortened form as "The Advent of the Whalebacks on the Great Lakes, *Nor'easter* 23, No. 5 (September–October 1998).

"Data Book" (Pittsburgh Steamship Company 1907 and 1908).

McDougall, "Account Book" (Superior Public Museums, Superior, WI).

McDougall, "Scrap Book and Photo Album, volumes 1–4" (Lake Superior Maritime Collection, Jim Dan Hill Library, University of Wisconsin-Superior).

"Mortgage No. a77271," (Mortgage Record, vol. 28, Douglas County, Wisconsin).

Thro, Ken, "Roster of Whaleback Ships with Launch Dates, Fates, and Principal Dimensions."

"U.S. Coast Guard Report of Vessel Casualty or Accident, Duluth, Minnesota" (November 22, 1969).

CORRESPONDENCE

American Steel Barge Company. "Souvenir Double Launching," Invitation to Attend the Launch of *Barge 107*. 1890. Superior Public Museums.

Letter of recommendation from Alexander McDougall for Robert Clarke dated November 23, 1896. Superior Public Museums.

Ida Strong to Ken Thro, May 10, 1987. Superior Public Museums.

The following correspondence from the American Steel Barge Company are available on microfilm #M33 at the Minnesota Historical Society, St. Paul.

Joseph L. Colby to Charles Wetmore, November 28, 1888.

Joseph L. Colby to Charles Wetmore, December 4, 1888.

Joseph L. Colby to Charles Wetmore, December 5, 1888.

Colgate Hoyt to Stockholders, December 14, 1892.

Colgate Hoyt to C. W. Wetmore, December 15, 1892.

Alexander McDougall to Colgate Hoyt, February 5, 1889.

Alexander McDougall to Colgate Hoyt, August 14, 1889.

Memorandum from C. W. Wetmore to American Steel Barge Co. Board of Directors, 1892.

Memorandum of Agreement between Alexander McDougall, Colgate Hoyt, and Charles W. Wetmore, December 1888. (Contract for organizing American Steel Barge Company.)

Joseph R. Oldham, Inland Lloyds Inspector to J. H. Colby, November 9, 1891.

FINANCIAL AND MISCELLANEOUS STATISTICAL REPORTS

The following financial and statistical data from the American Steel Barge Company are available on microfilm #M33 at the Minnesota Historical Society, St. Paul.

American Steel Barge Company, *Cash Flow Projections, July 1, 1892, September 15, 1892, and November 1, 1892.*

American Steel Barge Company, *Earnings as a Percentage of Present Value for Barges and Steamships* (undated).

American Steel Barge Company, *Estimated Net Earnings of Barge Carrying Flour or Package Freight as Compared with Wheat and Grain.*

American Steel Barge Company, *Extract of log* SS JOSEPH L. COLBY, *Voyage from Newport News, VA to Galveston, Texas,* August, 29 1892.

American Steel Barge Company, *Operating Statistics, 1892, For* J. L. COLBY, and BARGES 109, 110, 201, *and* 202, Percentage of Earnings on Cost and Present Value, 18.

American Steel Barge Company, *Season of 1892 Atlantic Service: Actual Earnings of Vessels.*

American Steel Barge Company, *Shareholder List,* undated.

American Steel Barge Company, *Statement of Earnings and Expenses, Oct. 31, 1892.*

American Steel Barge Company, *Statement of Earnings and Expenses of Barges during 1891.*

McDougall, Alexander, or Hoyt, Colgate, *Relative earnings of the different boats engaged in the Lake Superior trade compared with our own vessels,* 1895–1896.

INDEX

Italicized page numbers indicate illustrations. Italicized page numbers followed by the letter "*t*" indicate tables. "*Plate*" indicates an illustration in the gallery.

CPSIA information can be obtained
at www.ICGtesting.com
Printed in the USA
LVHW02*0828050418
572047LV00003B/5/P